CISTERCIAN FATHER

MW00475034

In the School of Love

CISTERCIAN FATHERS SERIES: NUMBER SIXTY-FOUR

In the School of Love

An Anthology of Early Cistercian Texts

Selected and annotated by Edith Scholl OCSO
Introduction by M. Basil Pennington OCSO

Cistercian Publications
Kalamazoo, Michigan — Spencer, Massachusetts

Cistercian Publications
Editorial Offices and Customer Service
Institute of Cistercian Studies
Western Michigan University
Kalamazoo, MI 49008

Warehouse and Distribution
Saint Joseph's Abbey
Spencer, MA 01562

British and European Customer Service
97 Loughborough Road
Thringstone, Coalville, Leics. LE67 8LQ

http://www.spencerabbey.org/cistpub/

The work of Cistercian Publications
is made possible in part
by support from Western Michigan University
to The Institute of Cistercian Studies

Typeset by BOOKCOMP, INC., Grand Rapids, Michigan
Printed by MCNAUGHTON & GUNN, Saline, Michigan

Table of Contents

May I love him whom to love is to live indeed.

William of Saint Thierry[1]

1. *On Contemplating God* 3; CF 3:40

Foreword

In the School of Love

*T*HE SCHOOL OF LOVE. Does love have to be taught? Or is love the teacher in this school? And where do we find such a school?

It is my hope that the texts assembled in this book will give answers to these questions. They have been taken from the writings of cistercian monks and nuns who lived in the twelfth and thirteenth centuries. These men and women believed that love did need to be taught, and that only Love can teach the art of loving. They thought of the monasteries in which they lived as a school in which they learned love and experienced a love that surpasses human understanding. Cistercians through the centuries—and those living today—agree.

The Cistercians[1] have become quite well known in recent years,—thanks to such writers as Thomas Merton, Basil Pennington, and Miriam Pollard, and to modern english translations of the works of cistercian writers from medieval times. The cistercian movement began in the year 1098, in the determination of a small group of monks in Burgundy, in southeastern France. They had a vision of a simpler, more authentic monastic life than they had experienced; a life conformed to the ancient Rule of Saint Benedict and yet adapted to the needs of their own times; a life of wholehearted search for God in poverty and solitude. These monks settled in a place called Cîteaux—in Latin *Cistercium*—from which they took their name. Their vision evidently corresponded to the aspirations of their contemporaries. It spread like wildfire; within fifty years the whole of Europe was dotted with hundreds of monasteries of men and women imbued with the same vision and striving to realize it in their lives. It has survived the vicissitudes of history, undergoing periods of decline, reform and regrowth. After nine hundred years it continues to grow and adapt itself to changing conditions; today more than seven thousand men and women throughout the world are part of the cistercian family.

This book concentrates on one aspect of the Cistercians' vision: their *spirituality*. Spirituality is presently something of an 'in' word, but its meaning often remains vague. For the purposes of this book, spirituality may be defined as concern with the deepest element of the human person, variously called the heart, the soul, or the spirit. This is the place where we encounter the transcendent, the divine; the place where we respond to the Spirit.

Cistercian spirituality, like all christian spirituality, is firmly rooted in Scripture and the tradition of the Church. Yet it has nuances and emphases all its own. Many of these have a special appeal for persons today. Cistercian spirituality stresses the experiential, the affective, as well as the rational. It is joyful, optimistic, balanced, practical. Above all, it is a spirituality of *love*. Love—what word is so overworked, misused, degraded, yet remains so fundamental and indispensable to a truly human life? Even more than spirituality, love eludes definition. In a moment we shall consider some of the ways the early Cistercians described it. But first, it is important that we realize that love is the alpha and the omega, the beginning and the end, of cistercian spirituality—indeed, the key to understanding it—because God *is* Love (1 Jn 4:16). Love is God's very being; the life of the Trinity is an exchange of love among the three Persons—a love that pours itself out in creation, in the redemptive incarnation, death, and resurrection of the Son of God, and in each and every human being, made in God's image and made to respond in kind, by loving. The Cistercians are convinced that we can only become what we are created to be by loving: loving God first and above all else, and also loving our neighbor as our self. Our love for God must be that we love him without measure; our love for neighbor requires a healthy love of ourselves and, ultimately, of all of God's creation.

When the Cistercians speak about love, they strike to the very heart of this inner human need:

Love's birthplace is God.
There it is born, there nourished, there developed.
There it is a citizen, not a stranger but a native.
Love is given by God alone, and it endures in him,
for it is due to no one else but him and for his sake.

William of Saint Thierry[2]

When God loves, he desires nothing but to be loved,
since he loves us for no other reason than to be loved,
for he knows that those who love
him are blessed in their very love.

Bernard of Clairvaux[3]

Love is a power of the soul,
leading her by a kind of natural gravity
to her place or destination.

William of Saint Thierry[4]

Love is the heart's palate
which tastes that God is sweet,
the heart's eye
which sees that God is good.
It is the place capable of receiving God, great as he is.
Someone who loves God grasps him.

Aelred of Rievaulx[5]

Love is sufficient for itself;
it gives pleasure in itself, and for its own sake.
It is its own merit, and its own reward.
Love needs no cause beyond
itself, nor does it demand fruits;
it is its own purpose.
I love because I love.
I love that I may love.

Bernard of Clairvaux[6]

This book takes us to the *school* of love. Our human
love has been turned back on itself, deflected from its
proper object. We have to be schooled. Our love has to be
reoriented, set free: 'Although love has been implanted
in the human soul by the Author of nature, in our present
condition it must be taught. It is not to be taught as if it
were something which no longer exists, but as something that needs to be purified and strengthened.'[7] The
Cistercians view the monastery as the school where this

re-education occurs, but its enrollment is not limited to monks and nuns; it is open to anyone who desires an 'education of the heart'.

Any school, of course, is only as good as its teachers. The cistercian school of love boasts a splendid faculty. The men and women whose writings are cited in this book were themselves students in this school before becoming teachers. The Lord Jesus has 'breathed on them and filled them with his Holy Spirit, so that they have understood how to speak in a way that pleases him.'[8] They can lead us to the one 'who holds the teacher's chair *par excellence* in the school of those who love Jesus': the virgin Mary.[9] Finally, in this school, it is God himself, it is Love, who teaches the art of love.[10] For though 'human beings may teach how to seek God and angels how to adore him, the Holy Spirit alone teaches how to find him, possess him and enjoy him.'[11]

This book does not pretend to be anything but an *introduction* to this school. In it readers will find an almost random selection from the great riches of the cistercian heritage. These passages have been chosen to highlight some characteristic and important themes and to give the reader a taste of cistercian spirituality. As much as possible I have let the Cistercians speak for themselves, adding a few comments of my own only where it seemed necessary to do so in order to bring out the significance of some particular text. To encourage further exploration, I have given the source of each selection, as well as a complete bibliography.

The word 'school' is derived from the latin *schola*, which has overtones of leisurely learning. *In the School of Love* is intended for leisurely, meditative reading—the kind of reading known as *lectio divina*. Father Basil Pennington describes *lectio* well in his introduction. I am deeply grateful to my community, and above all to my abbess, Mother Agnes Day, for affording me sufficient leisure to assemble these texts, as well as for their love and care over many years. My thanks also go to the Board of Directors of Cistercian Publications, especially Dr Rozanne Elder, Fr Basil Pennington, Dr John Sommerfeldt, and Dr Lawrence Cunningham, for their support, encouragement, and practical advice.

ES

Notes to Foreword

1. There are two Cistercian Orders in the Catholic Church: the Order of Cistercians and the Order of Cistercians of the Strict Observance, popularly known as 'Trappists' after a famous seventeenth-century french monastery which led a movement to recover the ideals of the early Cistercians and their models, the Desert Fathers. In addition, Congregations of Bernardine nuns trace their origins to the Cistercians and follow a cistercian spirituality.
2. *The Nature and Dignity of Love* 1; CF 30:53.
3. *On the Song of Songs*, 83.4; CF 40:184.
4. *The Nature and Dignity of Love*, Prologue 2; CF 30:47.
5. *The Mirror of Charity* 1.1.2; CF 17:88.
6. *On the Song of Songs*, 83.4; CF 40:184
7. William of Saint Thierry, *The Nature and Dignity of Love*, Prologue 2; CF 30:49.
8. John of Forde, Sermon 24.2; CF 39:135.
9. John of Forde, Sermon 14.4; CF 39:138–139.
10. Gertrud of Helfta, *Spiritual Exercises* 5; CF 49:83; Beatrice of Nazareth, *Seven Manners of Love,* Tjurunga (Australia) No. 50 (May 1996) 80.
11. William of Saint Thierry, *The Golden Epistle*, 264; CF 12:96.

Lectio and Love

An Introduction to the Cistercian Tradition

by

M. Basil Pennington ocso

*L*ECTIO IS A WORD whose time has come. It seems to be becoming an accepted english word—and that is good. There is an old saying: every translator is a traitor. We know how much can be lost in translation—and how the new word carries nuances of its own. Certainly if we translated *lectio* simply as 'reading' we would betray this latin word, losing its rich traditional connotations.

Lectio is a meeting with God in and through his Word. As in any intimate meeting, far more is communicated than the literal meaning of the words. God uses stories and images to invite us to be aware of our feelings in *lectio*. In this meeting with God in his Word, even though there is no question of body language complementing the spoken word, God is using human communication and intends to use it to the full.

Yet here another level of communication, that of the Spirit, is paramount. 'Eye has not seen, ear has not heard, nor has it entered into the human mind what God has prepared for those who love him but the Spirit makes it known to us.' (1 Cor 2:10) This, of course, is why it is important always to begin our *lectio*, as Saint Benedict directs, with earnest prayer, seeking the help of the Spirit. 'The Spirit will teach you all things and bring to mind all that I have told you', says the Lord. (Jn 14:26)

Equally important is a deep awareness of the presence of God in his Word. Catholics have always been very aware of the Real Presence of the Lord in the Eucharist. The Spirit, speaking through the Second Vatican Council used this long tradition in its teaching: just as the Lord is truly present in the Eucharist so is he present in the Bread of the Word. God nourishes us by both.

God is present in his Word and speaks to us. But how do we listen in *lectio*?

Historically, just after the era of the Cistercian Fathers, a great shift occurred in the way people read. Letters began to be organized by a visual arrangement that allowed meaning to be conveyed to the mind directly from the page through the eye. No longer did understanding depend on pronouncing the words aloud and hearing them with the ear. The full incarnational involvement of the person in the process of reading was significantly lessened. Whether this shift had as much impact on the way we read as did the scholastic approach, I do not know. But certainly there was a shift that greatly impoverished the practice of *lectio* and robbed it of its power to form in the reader the mind of Christ Jesus. Instead of letting the Word with all its mythopoetic power come into us and expand our consciousness and more and more extend the boundaries of our attentiveness to the Divine, instead of pondering these Words of Revelation in our hearts, we began to 'think them over', to fit them into our pre-established conceptual system. We collected beautiful ideas, insights, motives for action, but we were no longer gently led into that experience of the Divine which we call contemplation. We began to seek to be *informed* rather than *formed* by the Word. *Lectio* led not to contemplation but to action. In the process the christian community largely lost the contemplative dimension of the Christ-life.

One of the services the Cistercian Fathers and Mothers of the twelfth and thirteenth century render us is training us in *lectio*. They lived lives of intense *lectio* and profound contemplation before this pernicious shift impoverished christian spirituality. With their gentle tutelage, under their gentle guidance, we can hope to relearn the way of *lectio*, the way of reading that allows us to be formed more than informed, that allows the Word to open itself and expand our consciousness to be ever more receptive of the Divine.

When we come to *lectio* with the Cistercian Fathers and Mothers, it is as though three of us sit down together: our God who speaks to us through his Word; our Father or Mother who, as a wise, experienced teacher and a loving friend, helps us to hear; and ourselves. We know that the Words of Revelation, cast in a rich mythopoetic mode, are meant to convey far more than their literal and historical meaning. At the allegorical dimension, the words carry many levels of rich meaning. They call us to a personal and a communal response. They point us to the fulfillment that will respond to but go infinitely beyond all our aspirations. The Fathers and Mothers, not with the logic of the schools but in the tradition of the Fathers of the Church, open these dimensions to us and invite us to enter in and discover so much more than information. Where the mind leaves off, the heart goes yet further. The Cistercian Fathers and Mothers invite us into a 'School of Love', into the domain where the heart knows what the mind can never grasp.

Bernard of Clairvaux (1090–1153) is the schoolmaster in this School of Love. He was already very much the lover when he entered the monastery at Cîteaux in 1112, at the age of twenty-two. But thirty-eight years of loving service to his brothers as abbot of Clairvaux—Cîteaux's third daughter-house—as well as dramatic and exhausting service to the Church at large brought him to the fullness of Christlike love.

His dear friend, William of Saint Thierry (c.1085–1148), a benedictine abbot who became a Cistercian, may have influenced Bernard as profoundly as he was influenced by him. In their pursuit of love and of an understanding of the ways of love, as well as in their literary expression of those ways, they walked—or should we, with Saint Benedict, say, they ran—arm in arm.

Guerric of Igny (d. 1157) was more than a disciple. He entered Clairvaux to sit at Bernard's feet until, by Bernard's influence, he was elected abbot of Igny, near Rheims, in 1138. For eighteen years he passed on to his sons what he learned as a son. It was only on the eve of his death that he began to gather his lessons about love into a never-to-be-completed collection of sermons.

Aelred of Rievaulx (1110–1167) was also a disciple. Although he had less personal contact than the others with Bernard, who was his Father Immediate (as the abbot of the founding abbey was called), he nonetheless so reflected Bernard's spirit and teaching that Bernard ordered him to write *The Mirror of Charity*.

Gilbert of Hoyland (d. 1172) and John of Forde (d. 1214) were so formed by Bernard's teaching that they dared to continue the great master's commentary on the *Song of Songs*, bringing it to completion.

Isaac of Stella (d. 1178) and Baldwin of Forde (d. 1191), living later in the twelfth century, experienced only the afterglow of the great abbot of Clairvaux, but the cistercian life they shared and his enduring influence inspired them to a life and a literary expression that was distinctly similar.

Daughters — who became mothers — like Gertrud of Helfta (d. 1308) and Beatrice of Nazareth (d. 1268), lived later still, but the same can be said of them.

Sister Edith of Mount Saint Mary's Abbey, Wrentham, Massachusetts, is herself a daughter of Cîteaux and a Cistercian Mother of our day. She has gathered here some of the most beautiful strains of this great cistercian chorus to create a symphony which not only delights our hearts but powerfully invites us to enter more fully into the School of Love. The various movements draw us gently forward, chapter by chapter, along the ways of love to the 'Consummation of Love'.

May this brief introduction to the loving wisdom and wise loving of the Fathers and Mothers of the great cistercian tradition help us appreciate how much this twelfth and thirteenth century School of Love can aid us who live in these post-scholastic days to rediscover and to enter into the contemplative dimension of christian life through a *lectio* that allows the Divine Spirit of Love to expand and form our minds and hearts.

Saint Joseph's Abbey, Spencer
Feast of Saint Ann, 1998

The latin word *homo*, like the greek *anthropos*, means a single human being, without distinction of gender. It is used both to refer to a single person and in a collective sense to mean the human race. In several of the texts in this book, it means at one and the same time Adam as the primal human, the entire human race as a single entity, and the individual person. In these instances it has seemed best to translate it as 'man', no more suitable english word being available. Likewise, since most of these texts were written by monks writing for other monks, and taking into consideration the limitations of the english language, I have opted for the 'universal he' rather than some circumlocution.

On the other hand, the Cistercians, like other writers of earlier times, use soul, *anima*, for the spiritual centre of the human person. Since *anima* is feminine, feminine pronouns have been used, rather than the more impersonal 'it'.

1 ❧

The Mystery of God

Once we have chosen to enter this School of Love, how do we begin to learn about love? Love's birthplace is God, for God is love[1] and the source of all love. So let us begin with God, the loving God of whom the Cistercians speak from their own experience.

I have marveled at the depth of his wisdom. I have experienced his goodness and mercy. I have perceived the excellence of his glorious beauty, and when I contemplate all these things I am filled with awe and wonder at his manifold greatness.

Bernard of Clairvaux[2]

I have ascended to the highest in me, and look! the Lord is towering above that. In my curiosity I have descended to explore my lowest depths, yet I found him even deeper. If I looked outside myself, I saw him stretching beyond the furthest I could see; and if I looked within, he was yet further within. Then I knew the truth of what I had read, 'In him we live and move and have our being'.

Bernard of Clairvaux[3]

In the School of Love, God is not a philosoph-
ical abstraction, but a personal God. Yet even
so, the Cistercians are able to speak of him in
philosophical terms when occasion requires:

Who is God? Clearly no better answer occurs to me than, 'He who is.' He wished this to be answered of him; he taught this to Moses and urged him to say to the people, 'He who is has sent me to you.' Indeed, this is fitting; nothing is more appropriate for the eternity which God is.

If you should say of God anything: that he is good, or great, or blessed, or wise, or any such thing, it is summed up in this phrase which says, 'He is'. For his being is what all these things are. If you should add a hundred such attributes, you would not go beyond his essence. If you should say these things you would add nothing; if you should not say them, you would take nothing away. If you have already perceived how singular, how supreme his being is, do you not judge that by comparison whatever God is not, is non-being rather than being?

Again, what is God? That without which nothing exists. Just as nothing can exist without him, so he cannot exist without himself: he exists for himself, he exists for all, and consequently in some way he alone exists who is his own existence and that of all else.

What is God? The Beginning; this is the answer he gave of himself. Many things in the world are spoken of as beginnings, and this is in respect to what comes after them. Yet if you look back and see something which pre-cedes another, you will call that the beginning. There-fore, if you seek the true and absolute beginning, you must discover that which has no beginning. That from which everything began clearly had no beginning itself, for if it began, it must have begun from some source. For nothing begins from itself, unless someone thinks that something which does not exist can cause itself to be or that something existed before it came to be, but since reason approves of neither of these it is clear that nothing exists as its own beginning. Moreover, what had its beginning from another was not first. Therefore, the true beginning in no way had a beginning, but totally began from itself.

What is God? A being for whom the ages have neither approached nor departed, and yet are not coeternal.

What is God? 'From whom and through whom and in whom are all things.' From whom are all things through creation, not as from a source; through whom are all things, lest you think there is one who is the author and one who is the maker; in whom are all things, not as in a place but as in power. From which are all things as if from one beginning; the author of all; through whom are all things, lest we think the maker a second beginning; in whom are all things, lest a third reality be introduced, that of place. From whom are all things, not of whom, because God is not matter; he is the efficient not the material cause. In vain do philosophers seek the material: God had no need of matter. He did not seek a workshop or a craftsman. He made everything through himself, in himself. Out of what? Out of nothing; for if he made it from something, he did not make that and consequently did not make everything. Do not suppose that from his own uncorrupted and incorruptible substance he made so many things, for even if they are good, they are corruptible.

Do you ask: if all things are in him, where is he? I can answer nothing more inadequately than this: what place can contain him? Do you ask where he is not? I cannot even answer that. What place is without God? God is incomprehensible, but you have learned a great deal if you discovered this about him: that he is nowhere who is not enclosed in a place, and he is everywhere who is not excluded from a place. In his own sublime and incomprehensible way, just as all things are in him, so he is in all things. For as the Evangelist says, 'He was in the world.' Furthermore, we know that where he was before the world was made, there he is today. There is no need to ask further where he was: nothing existed except him, therefore he was in himself.

Bernard of Clairvaux[4]

God is the Being who is Perfection unlimited, who is Beauty without quality, Greatness without extension, Presence uncircumscribed by place, Existence beyond time.

Isaac of Stella[5]

. . . omnipotent will, benevolent virtue, eternal light, unchangeable reason, supreme blessedness.

Bernard of Clairvaux[6]

Of all God's qualities, the Cistercians dwell most often on the divine goodness, mercy, and kind-ness—all aspects of love:

You are he who is supremely good, goodness itself, the life of the hearts of men and the light of their inward eyes.

William of Saint Thierry[7]

. . . not only the generous giver, the liberal administrator, the kindest consoler and the watchful governor of my life, but above and beyond that, the richest redeemer, the eternal defender who enriches and glorifies.

Bernard of Clairvaux[8]

God's love is rich and opulent, for where did all the mercies which we have received from God come from if not from his continual kindness, his unmitigated liberality, his pure grace, his full and perfect benevolence?

Baldwin of Forde[9]

The love of God with which he loved us before the foundation of the world and chose us in his beloved Son is itself the source and origin of all the good things which were bestowed upon us on the day of our creation, the day of our redemption, and the day of our justification and sanctification. But in addition to these, it is also the source of the things which will be bestowed upon us on the day of our glorification, when God will be glorified in us and we in him.

God did not love us insignificantly or indifferently or meagerly, but fully and richly; not with a feigned or false love, but purely and sincerely; not just in appearance, not just outwardly, as though it were only on the surface, but inwardly, from the bottom of his heart; not in word and tongue, but in deed and truth.

If you want to know the extent of this love, its greatness is such that only God can measure it; as far as we are concerned, it is immense and immeasurable. If it were possible for us to comprehend its extent in some way with all the saints, it is so great that we can comprehend it only with the greatest difficulty—although in reality [its comprehension] is wholly beyond our abilites. Its height and depth, its length and its breadth are beyond anything we can describe or conceive.

Its height is the sublimity of glory which God has prepared for those who love him, the glory, that is, which the eye has not seen, nor the ear heard, and which has not arisen in the heart of man. Its depth is the emptying of himself by the only-begotten Son of God and the descent of such majesty from the bosom of the Father to the shame of the cross, from the source of life to the end of life, from the highest point to the lowest, from heaven to hell, from one extremity to the other. Who is able to conceive these two extremes? Who can comprehend the height from which he came, or the vast distance between the summit from which he descended and the lowest depths to which he descended? The height of this love, therefore, is the ennobling of mankind; its depth is God's descent into this world—a descent which, as we have said, was from the highest point to the lowest, from the beginning to the end.

Its length, however, has neither beginning nor end. Just as his love for us has no ending, neither does it have any beginning, for the mercy of the Lord is from eternity to eternity upon them that fear him. Its breadth is wide and far-reaching and shows itself in the way in which his benevolence and kindness are of universal benefit. The benefit of his benevolence is that he wants everyone to be saved and come to the knowledge of the truth; that of his kindness is that he did not even spare his own Son, but delivered him up for us all. It is his kindness, however, which we should value more highly because it extends not only *to* all things, but *through* all things, for in giving us his only Son has he not also given us all things with him?

Baldwin of Forde[10]

This God is a single Being and a loving community, a Trinity of Persons: Father, Son, and Holy Spirit.

Father, Son and Holy Spirit are names of goodness, names of gentleness, sweetness and love. Who is more gentle than the Father, who so great, kind and merciful? Who is dearer than Jesus Christ? Our savior is all healing, all goodness, gentleness, sweetness. Who is more loving, dear and holy than the Holy Spirit? He is the love of the Father and the Son, and by him all who are made holy receive sanctification.

A twelfth-century Cistercian[11]

These Divine Persons are all involved, out of love, in our human history.

Let us consider ourselves, and the actions of the Trinity in us, from the beginning of the world until the end.

Let us see how that Majesty upon whom lie both the administration and the governance of the ages has been concerned not to lose us forever. Indeed he had made all things mightily, and he was governing all things wisely. There was goodness in God as well, goodness great beyond measure; but it lay concealed in the heart of the Father, to be lavished at a seasonable time upon the race of the children of Adam.

His own kindness induced the Word of God, who was on high, to come down to us; his compassion drew him; the truth by which he had promised that he would come compelled him; the purity of a virginal womb received him; virtue reared him; obedience steered him in all things; patience armed him; and charity revealed him by words and miracles.

He gave us his life to instruct us, his death to destroy ours, his resurrection to herald ours, his ascension to prepare for ours, and finally his Spirit to assist us in our weakness. This Spirit gives us the pledge of salvation, the force of life, and the light of knowledge. He is the sweet and gentle Spirit who bends our will, or rather straightens and directs it more fully toward his own so that we may be able to understand his will truly, love it fervently, and fulfill it effectually.

Bernard of Clairvaux[12]

> *So loving and generous a God cannot simply be regarded with indifference, or be a matter for dispassionate, rational speculation. The Cistercians, therefore, are far readier to speak to God than about God:*

Now, therefore, Lord, in complete faith I worship you. You who are God, the one Cause of all that is, the Wisdom whence the wiseness of every wise person comes, the Gift whence every happy person derives his happiness.

William of Saint Thierry[13]

I love you, Lord, my powerful defender, wise guide, gentle consoler, generous rewarder. Confident, I cast all my care on him whose strength cannot be overthrown, whose wisdom cannot be led astray, whose loving kindness cannot be exhausted in fulfilling my every need.

Guerric of Igny[14]

God is the meditation of my heart and my inheritance, that I await, long for and delight in. He is the objective I have set myself, the whole reason for my efforts. He, God himself, is the inheritance I plan to bring to a home of right-ordered love, that he may sup with me and I with him. He is ever in my thoughts, he is my heart's delight. I seek him, the transcendent, for his own sake. By him, the immanent, I feed on him. He is both the field I work and the food I work for. He is both reason and reward of all I do, my beginning and end without end. Forever he is mine; eternally my inheritance.

Isaac of Stella[15]

My soul, say to God: 'Who are you, Lord, that I may know you?' You alone are what you are and who you are, that is, that than which nothing greater can be thought, nor anything better, nor more joyful. You are life, wisdom, light, truth, goodness, eternity, the one whom all need that they may exist and be happy. My soul, you have found what you were seeking; you were seeking God and you have found him to be the highest of all, that than which nothing greater can be thought, and this is life, wisdom, light, truth, goodness, eternal beatitude, blessed eternity and all that is good. God the Father, this good is you, and this good is also your Word, that is, your Son; for you are simple, and what is born of you is yourself. There is one love and communion between you and your Son which is the Holy Spirit who proceeds from you both. Nothing can proceed from that which is most simple other than itself.

A twelfth-century Cistercian.[16]

You, therefore, God the Father,
  by whom as Creator we live,
You Wisdom of the Father,
  by whom we have been made anew and taught to
    live wisely,
You, Holy Spirit, whom and in whom we love,
  and so live happily, and are to live yet more so,
You, who are Three in one Substance, the one God,
  from whom we are,
  by whom we are,
  in whom we are,
You, from whom we departed by sinning,
  to whom we were made unlike,
  but away from whom we have not been allowed to
    perish,
You, the Beginning, to whom we are returning,
  the Pattern we are following,
  the Grace by which we are reconciled,
You we worship and bless!
  To you be glory for ever!
    Amen.

William of Saint Thierry[17]

Sources and Scriptural References

1. *The Golden Epistle* 25; CF 12:18.
   Gen 32:30, 1 Cor 13:12, 1 Jn 3:2.
2. *On Loving God* 1; CF 13:93.
3. 1 Jn 3:8
4. *On the Song of Songs*, 74.6; CF 40:91.
   Qo 7:25; Ps 18:13; Eph 4:23; Ps 49:2; Ps 50:2.
5. *On the Song of Songs*, 74.5.
   Acts 17:28.
6. *Five Books on Consideration*, 5.13–14; CF 37:155–7.
   Ex 3:14; Jn 1:3; Jn 8:25; Rom 11:36.
7. *Sermons on the Christian Year*, Sermon 4.11; CF 11:32.
8. *Five Books on Consideration*, 5.24; CF 37:169.
9. *On Contemplating God* 2; CF 3:37.
10. *On Loving God*, 14; CF 13:107.
11. *Spiritual Tractate* 13; CF 41:131.
12. *Tractate* 13; CF 41:131–133
13. 'The Spirit and the Soul', in *Three Treatises on Man*, CF 24:267.
14. Second Sermon for Pentecost 2–8; in *Sermons for the Summer Season*, CF 53:75–80.
15. *On Contemplating God* 13; CF 3:63.
16. Sermon 23.3, in *Liturgical Sermons*; CF 32:11–12.
17. Sermon 5.13; CF 11:41.
18. 'On the Spirit and the Soul', in *Three Treatises on Man*, CF 24:281.
19. *On Contemplating God* 13; CF 3:63–64.

2

The Human Condition

Who are the students in this school of love? We are—ordinary human beings, with all the usual strengths and weaknesses. And if we are ever to learn to know and love God, we must also learn to know ourselves. The Cistercians have a very positive view of human nature, and this fundamental conviction of our value radiates in all their writings. They cry out to us to 'acknowledge our dignity, the glory of our human nature'[1]. We are noble creatures; we have an inborn worth which gives us imperial and regal dignity; we have a capability for greatness, a capacity for the eternal—for God himself.

WHAT AN EXCELLENT CREATURE is a human being! He is capable of eternal blessedness and the glory of our great God. By his breath he was created, with his likeness he has been stamped, and by his blood he has been redeemed: he has been endowed with faith, adopted in the Spirit.

Bernard of Clairvaux[2]

The soul is capable of righteousness, wisdom, truth, and she yearns for them; that perhaps is why she is said to be made in the image of God. She is a lofty creature, in her capacity for greatness, and in her longing we see a token of her uprightness.

Bernard of Clairvaux[3]

What a capacity the soul has, how privileged her merits, that she is found worthy not only to receive the divine presence, but to be able to make sufficient room!

Bernard of Clairvaux[4]

What is the source of our innate greatness? That God has created us to his own image and likeness.

O image of God, recognize your dignity; let the effigy of your Creator shine forth in you. Purify yourself, train yourself in godliness, and you shall find the kingdom of God within you. To yourself you seem of little worth, but in reality you are precious. Be wholly present to yourself and employ yourself wholly in knowing yourself and knowing whose image you are, and likewise in discerning and understanding what you are and what you can do in him whose image you are.

William of Saint Thierry[5]

Deep within ourselves, if we listen, we can hear God cry out to the soul:

Know yourself to be my image; thus you can know me, whose image you are, and you will find me within you.

William of Saint Thierry[6]

To this end alone were we created and do we live: to be like God; for we were created in his image. Resemblance to God is the whole of our perfection. Not to choose to be perfect is to fall short.

To this resemblance which is human perfection,
there are, however, various degrees:

There is a likeness to God which is lost only with life itself, left to everyone by the Creator of all as evidence of a better and more sublime likeness. As far as merit is concerned, this likeness to God in us is of no importance with God, since it derives from nature, not from will or effort.

But there is another likeness, one closer to God, inasmuch as it is freely willed. It consists in the virtues and inspires the soul as it were to imitate the greatness of Supreme Good by the greatness of her virtue, and his unchangeable eternity by her unwearying perseverance in good.

In addition to this there is yet another likeness. It is so close in its resemblance that it is styled not merely a likeness but unity of spirit. It makes us one with God, one spirit, not only with the unity which comes of willing the same thing but with a greater fullness of virtue: the inability to will anything else.

William of Saint Thierry[7]

Their intense awareness of having been made in
God's image and likeness leads the Cistercians
to respond in gratitude.

O good Creator! How well you created me! How glori-
ously you fashioned me! How blessed a place you appointed for my dwelling! You created me, Lord, for the
good works you had prepared for me to walk in, as the
Apostle says. You fashioned me in your own image and
likeness, and set me in the paradise of your delight, that
I might till it and guard it. You who have made us, bring
us to perfection; perfect in us the image and likeness of
yourself for which you made us.

William of Saint Thierry[8]

Our 'capacity for God', as the Cistercians call
it, our ability somehow to bear God within our-
selves, is born in us. Its realization is, in fact,
the very purpose for which we were created:

We are the only creature capable of embracing the God
who in the very greatness of his generosity has become
the Gift to be shared and enjoyed.

Isaac of Stella[9]

We were created to the image of God for this purpose,
that, devoutly mindful of God in order to understand
him, humbly understanding him in order to love him
and loving him with ardor and wisdom until we attain
to possession and fruition of him, we might be rational

animals. For this is to fear God and keep his commandments, which is our whole duty. And this is the image
and likeness of God in us.

William of Saint Thierry[10]

Our proper occupation is knowing and loving God, and,
not least, delighting in such knowledge and love. We
have been made in the image and likeness of God for the
sake of this knowledge and love; and by means of them
we are made new and formed again to God's image and
likeness: through understanding to the image, through
form of life to the likeness. Yet notice: in order to be
formed again and come to share God's nature we must
first shape our life according to Christ's.

Isaac of Stella[11]

*God has given us faculties by which to respond
to him. These are our ability to reason, our
memory, and our freedom to choose:*

Minds endowed with reason are the first and only beings
made in God's image, thanks to the gift God willed to
make of his Joy. They are for that reason the only creatures capable of sharing his knowledge and love. Their
intellects and wills, faculties that enable them to understand and to love, fit them to share God's communicable
nature. These faculties are, as it were, receptacles and
tools belonging to their nature that the first gift of grace
puts in being and the further gift of grace fills against
both emptiness and the wrong kind of content. Wrong

notions and misdirected love may occupy them with evil; God alone, their author and purpose, can satisfy them.

Isaac of Stella[12]

We were created with free will and willing freedom, creatures noble in God's eyes.

Bernard of Clairvaux[13]

Free choice is something clearly divine which shines forth in the soul like a jewel set in gold. From it the soul derives its power of judgment, and its option of choosing between good and evil, between life and death, in fact between light and darkness, and any other concepts which are perceived by the soul as opposites. It is the eye of the soul which as censor and arbiter exercises discrimination and discernment between these things, and arbiter in discerning and free in choosing. It is called free choice because it is exercised in these matters in accordance with the freedom of the will. By it a person can acquire merit; everything you do, whether good or ill, which you had the choice of doing or not doing, is duly imputed to you for merit or censure. It is only we humans who have not been dominated by nature, therefore we alone among living creatures are free.

Bernard of Clairvaux[14]

This human freedom, as great a gift as it is, is not without its risks:

Our first parents were endowed with free will and aided by God's grace. By a lasting love of this same God, they could have delighted everlastingly in the memory and knowledge of God and been everlastingly happy. But they could also divert this love to something less, and so by withdrawing from God's love begin to grow old and deliver themselves up to misery. Now for a creature endowed with reason, there is no other happiness than to cling to God.

Aelred of Rievaulx[15]

The constant and repeated generosity of God moved the Cistercians to gratitude and praise:

Among the blessings of God some are the blessings of creation, others of restoration, and others of day-to-day consolation. The blessings of creation are that we were created in the image and likeness of God, that in him we live and move and have our being and are his offspring, and that by his gift we have a soul and body and all the senses of soul and body in their full number and completeness. Whatever good things we possess as a result of our creation, these we receive by God's generosity, and all these good things of ours are nothing but gifts of God.

The blessings of restoration are the sacrament of the incarnation, the mystery of the passion of Christ, and all the sacraments which Christ took upon himself for us or which he instituted for us to receive. Such are the sacrament of the body and blood of Christ, the sacrament of baptism, and all the other sacraments of the Church by which the merciful God has bestowed grace and power for the remission of sins and the salvation of believers.

The blessings of everyday consolation are those which the Father of mercies and the God of all consolation, who consoles us in all our tribulation, accords us in his mercy day by day. Our Father knows all that we need; we, I say, his unjust servants who, by his condescension, are yet his children. From our Father himself we receive the power to desire, to ask, and to hope. From him we can look for relief from all our sufferings, support in all our needs, and the remedy for all our infirmities. To whom shall we look for all these things, if not to him? 'Where does my help come from?' asks the prophet. 'My help is from the Lord, who made heaven and earth.'

See how the Lord has done great things for us! He over-whelms us with the multitude of his blessings and by his blessings strives to wrest from us our love. Surely God should be loved with our whole heart because of these great and manifold blessings! It is only right and proper and just that we should give our heart to him if he himself thinks fit to ask for it. And he *has* thought it fit! 'Give me your heart', he says to us! He who asks you to give him your heart wants to be loved from the heart. God wants our whole heart for himself, that in him, before all else, it may take its pleasure.

Baldwin of Forde[16]

Let us give thanks to our Maker, our Benefactor, our Redeemer, our Rewarder, to him who is our hope. He is our rewarder; he is our reward, nor should we expect from him anything save himself. In the first place, he preserves us; we are his; for it is he who made us, and not we ourselves. Does it seem to you a little thing that he made you? Think of what quality he made you. For even with regard to your body he made you a noble creature; and still more so with regard to your soul, inasmuch as you are the extraordinary image of the Creator, sharing his rationality, capable of eternal happiness. In both body and soul man is the most admirable of all creatures, being integrated with himself by the incomprehensible ingenuity and unsearchable wisdom of the Creator. We are then as great as this gift itself.

Bernard of Clairvaux[17]

Why should the soul not venture with confidence into the presence of him by whose image she sees herself honored, and in whose likeness she knows herself made glorious? Why should she fear a majesty when her very origin gives her ground for confidence? All she has to do is to take care to preserve her natural purity by innocence of life, or rather to study to beautify and adorn with the brightness of her actions and dispositions the glorious beauty which is her birthright.

Why then do we not set to work? There is a great natural gift within us, and if it is not allowed full play the rest of our nature will go to ruin, as though it were being eaten away by the rust of decay. This would be an insult to its Creator.

Bernard of Clairvaux[18]

We were created for you by yourself,
and towards you our face is set.
We acknowledge you our maker and creator;
we adore your wisdom and pray
that it may order all our life.
We adore your goodness and mercy, and
beg them ever to sustain and help us.

William of Saint Thierry[19]

*Yet for all their gratitude, the Cistercians are re-
alistically aware of another side to our human
nature:*

'I have grown old among all my enemies', and I am
not speaking only of those enemies who are outside
me, those among whom I dwelt when I dwelt with the
inhabitants of Cedar. I refer now more to those enemies
who are within me, who inhabit the land of my heart
and the land of my flesh. Canaanites and Jebusites and
Perezites are dwelling there, and they have become my
enemies. I myself, evil and unjust, am so much my own
enemy that I can as easily pray for myself as against
myself and say, 'Deliver me, O Lord, from the evil man;
rescue me from the unjust man.' Deliver me, O Lord,
from myself, for after you, O Lord, there is none that I
should fear as much as myself. Who can lie in ambush
for my soul as I can? Who is so opposed to my salvation
as I am? Who is as skilled in achieving my destruction as
myself? Who can coax and lure me to my ruin as I can?
Who seeks my soul to take it away? Who thinks to rob
me of my reward? Who is there, Lord, who tries as hard
as I to sweep away that splendid inheritance which you
have promised? Who is there more than I who hates my
soul with so hostile a hatred?

Baldwin of Forde[20]

No wonder they ask themselves: 'How did such
faintheartedness and such miserable abjection
come to be in so excellent a creature?'[21] *It came
about because we have turned away and withdrawn from God:*

Not by the stride of my foot, I think, Lord, but by the attachment of my mind. Unwilling to keep my soul's substance for you, I took it for myself, and wishing to possess myself without you, I lost both you and myself. See what a burden I have become to myself! I became a place of gloom and misery for myself, a place of horror and a region of destitution.

Aelred of Rievaulx[22]

We have descended from 'the region of likeness'—
our original likeness to God—into 'a region of
unlikeness':

You fashioned me in your own image and likeness, and set me in the paradise of your delight, that I might till it and guard it, till it with my good endeavors, and guard it, lest the serpent should steal in. The serpent did steal in, seduced me, and made me a sinner. For that reason I am driven out of the paradise of good conscience, and made to be an exile in a foreign country, the land of unlikeness.

William of Saint Thierry[23]

We are as if we were not, likened to vanity and counted as nothing, supposing ourselves to be something when actually we are nothing. We enter this world wounded, walk here and then depart, wounded still. There is no sound flesh in us, from the sole of the foot to the top of the head. Reflecting on the sad state of human nature, the prophet exclaims: 'A heavy yoke is upon the sons of Adam from the day they leave their mother's womb until they are buried in our common mother earth'.

Bernard of Clairvaux[24]

Our situation is, in biblical terms, like that of the man who went down from Jerusalem to Jericho and fell among robbers. It is like that of the prodigal son, the lost sheep, the lost coin:

Never would the Lord of mercy have allowed man to fall into such cruel hands had not man by his own personal and conscious wickedness first deserted him to whom he should have looked for strength. Man forsook God, man went his way down, and because he went down, he was forsaken by him who did not go down.

Forsaken by God, man fell into the power of him to whom such power was permitted, the devil. He showed no pity, but robbed, wounded, and left him half-dead. He who is altogether dying left man half-dead, in other words half-alive. And such is the life of mortal man: a living dying.

Mortal man, then, is left half-dead—though alive, he tends inevitably towards death—though dead, he is open to cure. They wounded him, the Gospel tells us. We must look into this, see what these wounds are, even if our situation teaches us what it means far better than any explanation. In addition to the weaknesses and afflictions of the body, themselves past all numbering, the wounds inflicted on and infecting mankind, in and from our first parents, are of seven kinds, of many species, and beyond all counting. The infections that stem from original sin and afflict us all are only seven, but they beget a way-ward, viper-like brood that caters to all sorts of sinful tendencies.

These are poisonous shoots that spring up in great pro-fusion, incentives to sin, demon's lairs, cradles of death.

The very first of these infections, first in the number of vices, first in degree of wickedness, first to be met with on the downward road is pride. Pride is an infatuation with one's own importance. As far as it may, it covets equality with the Most High. Disdaining to share the credit for its good deeds with anyone else, it gives birth to its firstborn, envy. The self-complacent cannot help being envious. What is envy but dread of another's success?

This in its turn, is followed by anger, a kind of mental derangement; you just cannot quietly consider the person you envy. Once anger establishes itself it produces deep depression, which once it has really taken hold of its dependent victim, plunges him into the depths of despair. There he is welcomed by avarice which is another name for love of this world. When you have no better world to hope for, the blandishments of avarice bring calm and comfort. Avarice soon shares its conquest with gluttony to the tune of: 'Come now, you have goods in plenty laid up for many years to come, eat and drink'. Gluttony devours him and then lust digests him.

Behold how the man who does not understand his true honor is compared to brute beasts, even unclean beasts, and becomes like them. Pride stole him from God, envy from his neighbor, anger from himself. Sadness threw him to the ground; avarice bound him; gluttony devoured him; lust made him dung. Such are the vices that besiege the soul.

Isaac of Stella[25]

I am that prodigal son who took to himself his share of the inheritance, for I did not wish to preserve my

strength for you and set out for a distant land, the region of unlikeness, behaving as one of the dumb beasts
and made like them. There I squandered all I owned
in riotous living and so I began to feel want. Unhappy
want, not only lacking bread but unable even to profit by
the food of pigs. Following the most unclean of animals I
wandered in the desert, in a waterless country, searching
in vain for the way to a city I could dwell in. Hungry and
thirsty, my soul wasted away in suffering.

Aelred of Rievaulx[26]

The fall affected the image of God in which we
were created and the consequences of this fall
therefore involve the created image in us, our
faculties of memory, reason and will:

By abusing free choice, man diverted his love from the
changeless good, God, and, blinded by his own self-
centeredness, he directed his love to what was inferior.
Thus withdrawing from the true good and deviating
toward what of itself was not good, where he anticipated
gain he found loss, and by perversely loving himself he
lost both himself and God.

Thus it very justly came about that someone who sought
the likeness of God in defiance of God, the more he
wanted to become similar to God out of curiosity, the
more dissimilar he became through self-centeredness.

Therefore, the image of God became disfigured in man
without becoming wholly destroyed. Consequently man

has memory—but it is subject to forgetfulness, under-standing—but it is open to error, and love which is prone to self-centeredness.

Aelred of Rievaulx[27]

This turning away from God, this fall from our original human dignity, involves us in an inner contradiction:

By the sin of disobedience man began to be at odds both with God and with himself, and by the just judgment of God, he who did not want peace with God did not find peace in himself. As it is written, 'You have set me against you, and I am become a burden to myself'. Man, therefore, who did not wish to be united with God, is divided in himself, for disobedience separates the soul from God and is the death of the soul.

Baldwin of Forde[28]

As a result of the fall, our soul has been im-printed with a different form—or rather defor-mity—for 'the soul that is unlike God is unlike itself as well'.[29]

If someone strives for peace in others while not being in accord with himself, with whom can he be in accord? With whom can he be in harmony, if he is at variance with himself, inconsistent with himself, always quar-relling with himself, and always contrary to himself? With whom can he be at peace if he is always disturbed and unquiet, like the raging of the sea which is never at rest? 'There is no peace for the wicked, says the Lord'.

Baldwin of Forde[30]

The blind perversity of our misery is lamentable indeed. Although we desire happiness ardently, not only do we not do those things by which we may obtain our desire but rather, with contrary disaffection, take steps to add to our misery. In my opinion, we would never do this, if a false image of happiness were not deceiving us, or a semblance of real misery frightening us off from happiness. Does anyone not see that poverty, grief, hunger, and thirst are no slight part of misery? Yet through them real misery is frequently averted and eternal happiness pursued.

Under the hue of happiness we grasp at real unhappiness, the false joy which does not escape real sorrow, preferring that to the misery which presages true happiness. We are like sick persons who earnestly hope to recover but because of the immediate pain shun an amputation or dread cauterization.

We are miserable, or deceived, as long as we think that happiness is something it is not, or are allured by the agreeableness of present things that fool us. We get used to misery, and indeed never lose our longing for happiness; and, as if struggling unhappily in this circle, never rest.

Aelred of Rievaulx[31]

Everyone who becomes aware of this situation and longs to be delivered from this inner contradiction cries out:

Unhappy creature that I am, who will free me from
this body of death by which I am weighed down and
oppressed to the extent that, unless the Lord helps me,
my soul would soon be living in hell! The soul struggling
under this load laments saying: 'Why have you set me
against you, and I am become a burden for myself?' By
the words 'I am become a burden for myself' is shown
that she herself is her own law and that nobody but
herself did that. But what she said previously, speaking
to God: 'Why have you set me against you?' means that
she has not escaped from God's law.

It is proper to God's eternally just law that the one who
does not want to accept its sweet rule, will be the slave
of his own will as a penance; he who casts away the
pleasant yoke and light load of charity, will have to bear
unwillingly the unbearable burden of his own will. By
a mysterious and just measure the eternal law has set its
fugitive against himself yet retaining him captive, for he
can neither escape the law of justice which he deserves
nor remain with God in his light, rest, and glory, because
he is subject to power and banished from happiness. O
Lord, my God, why do you not take away my sin, and
wherefore do you not remove my evil, that delivered
from the heavy load of self-will, I may breathe under
charity's light burden, that I may not be forced on by
slavish fear or drawn on by a hireling's cupidity? May I
be moved by your Spirit, the Spirit of liberty by which
your sons are acting, which bears witness to my spirit
that I, too, am one of your sons, that there is just one law
for both of us, that I must also be as you are in this world.

Bernard of Clairvaux[32]

I come to your feet, most loving Father. Behold, my sins
have made a separation between you and me. Ah! Have

mercy on me according to the multitude of your mercy, break the wall of my old way of life which keeps me from you; and draw me so vehemently toward you that I may, in the gentleness of your inextinguishable cherishing-love, wisely follow you by loving.

Lovingly-kind Jesus, although the will to do what is good is in me, I do not find the strength to accomplish it. Therefore, by the co-operation of your grace and through the spotless law of your love, turn my soul from the frailty of the human condition toward you in such a way that I may untiringly run the way of your commandments and cling inseparably to you. Be with me, my Lord, aiding me always and making me strong in the work that I have taken up for the love of your love.

Gertrud of Helfta[33]

Sources and Scriptural References

1. Bernard of Clairvaux, *Second Sermon for Christmas* 1; translation forthcoming in CF 51.
2. *On Conversion* 15; CF 25:49.
   Tt 2:13.
3. *On the Song of Songs* 80.2; CF 40:146.
4. *On the Song of Songs* 27.10; CF 7:83.
5. *Exposition on the Song of Songs* 66; CF 6:53.
6. *Exposition on the Song of Songs* 64; CF 6:51.
7. *The Golden Epistle* 259–262; CF 12:95.
   Gn 1:26.
8. *Meditation* 4.6; CF 3:113.
   Eph 2:10; Gn 1:26; Gn 2:15.
9. Sermon 32.10; translation forthcoming.
10. *Exposition on the Song of Songs* 88; CF 6:72.
    Qo 12:13.

11. Sermon 16.15–16; CF 11:134.
    Gn 1:26.
12. Sermon 26.1–2; CF 11:211.
13. *On Grace and Free Choice* 7; CF 11:211.
14. *On the Song of Songs* 81.6–7; CF 40:162–163.
15. *The Mirror of Charity* 1.4.11; CF 17:92.
16. Tractate 3; CF 38:82–83.
    Acts 17:28; 2 Cor 1:3–4; Ps 121:1–2; Prov 23:26.
17. *Sermons on Psalm 90* 14.1; CF 25:229.
    Ps 100:2; Gen 1:26; Rom 11:33.
18. *On the Song of Songs* 83.1–2; CF 40:181.
19. *Meditation* 1.3; CF 3:90.
20. Tractate 11; CF 41:94–95.
    Ps 6:8; Ps 140:1; Ps 40:17; Ps 62:4.
21. Bernard of Clairvaux, *On Conversion* 15; CF 25:49.
22. *The Mirror of Charity* 1.7.23; CF 17:99–100.
    Jb 7:20.
23. *The Mirror of Charity* 1.4.12; CF 17:93.
24. *Meditation* 4.6; CF 3:113.
    Gn 2:15; Ps 137:4.
25. Occasional Sermon 42.2; translation forthcoming.
    Is 40:17; Gal 6:3; Si 40:1.
26. Sermon 6.2–7; CF 11:48–49.
    Lk 10:30; Ps 40:6; Heb 12:15; Ph 2:6; Lk 12:19.
27. *On Jesus at the Age of Twelve* 3; CF 2:6–7.
    Lk 15:11–32; Ps 63:2; Ps 107:4.
28. *The Mirror of Charity* 1.4.12; CF 17:93.
29. Tractate 4; CF 38:114.
    Jb 7:20.
30. Bernard of Clairvaux, *On the Song of Songs* 82.4–5; CF 40:174–176.
31. Tractate 4; CF 38:111.
    Is 57:20; Is 48:22.
32. *The Mirror of Charity* 1.22.63–4; CF 17:123–124.
33. *On Loving God* 36; CF 13:128–129.
    Rom 7:24; Ps 94:17; Jb 7:20; Mt 11:30; Jb 7:21; Rom 8:14; 2 Cor 3:17; Rom 8:16; 1 Jn 4:17.
34. Exercise 4; CF 49:67.
    Ps 51:1; Is 5:5; Ps 119:32.

3

Turning Back to God

However deplorable the human separation from God, from Being, from Love, it is not irreparable. The prodigal son can return from the region of unlikeness to his Father's house. The Wisdom of God, Christ, has come to bind up the wounds of the man who fell among robbers, to find the coin lost by the housewife. Even though we have become alienated from God and from ourselves, our original integrity can be restored. The likeness to God in which we were made has only been obscured, not destroyed. Through love, it can be restored.

UNLIKENESS MEANS, not that the likeness has been destroyed, but that it has been concealed by something else which has been laid over it. The soul has not in fact put off her original form but has put on one foreign to her. The latter is an addition; the former has not been lost. This addition can hide the original form, but it cannot blot it out. The simplicity of the soul remains unshaken in its fundamental being, but it is not seen because it is covered by the disguise of human deception, pretense, and hypocrisy.

Bernard of Clairvaux[1]

To restore this likeness, to enable us to recover our likeness to God, Christ, the true Image, the Wisdom of the Father, came to us and became one of us.

Created as we were to the image and likeness of the Creator, we fell through our sin from God into ourselves, and fell from ourselves beneath ourselves into such an abyss of unlikeness that no hope was left. But there came the Son of God, eternal Wisdom; he bowed his heavens and came down. He made of himself a being who should be among us and like to us, so that we might grasp him; and he made us to be like to himself, so that we might be exalted by him.

William of Saint Thierry[2]

The image would have lain stained and deformed, had not the woman of the Gospel lit her lamp—had not Wisdom appeared in the flesh, in other words—, swept the house—of the vices— searched carefully for her lost coin—her image—which, its original luster gone, coated over with the skin of transgression, lay buried as it were in the dust; having found it, had she not wiped it clean and taken it away from the 'region of unlikeness;' then, refashioned in its erstwhile beauty made it like the saints in glory; were she not, indeed, some day to make it quite conformable to herself.

Who was better suited to this task than the Son of God? That very Form came, therefore, to which free choice was to be conformed, because in order that it might regain its original form, it had to be reformed from that out of which it had been formed.

Bernard of Clairvaux[3]

How marvelous a condescension in God
to come down from heaven in quest of us!
And how great an honor to us
so to be sought by God!

Bernard of Clairvaux[4]

Christ is the good Samaritan who rescues us as
well as the physician who binds up our wounds:

With what oil abounding was Christ anointed! From his bounty he poured oil into all our wounds! Yes, we are the wounded man who went down to Jericho, fell among brigands, was robbed, and wounded and left half dead. Too many passed by and there was not one to save his life. That great patriarch Abraham passed by, for he was not the one to justify but only justified through faith in the one to come. Moses passed by, for he was not the giver of grace but the lawgiver, giver of that Law which leads no one to the perfect one. For justice does not come from the Law. Aaron passed by. The priest passed by, and by the same victims which he offered unceasingly he was unable to 'cleanse men's consciences from dead works to serve the living God'. Patriarch, pontiff and prophet passed by, as barren in spirit as in deed; indeed, in the wounded man they also were wounded.

At the sight of the wounded only that true Samaritan is moved with compassion, is all compassion; he poured oil into wounds, himself into hearts, cleansing by faith the hearts of all.

Gilbert of Hoyland[5]

The physician comes to the sick, the redeemer to the captives, the way to the wanderers, life to the dead; he comes who will cast all our sins into the bottom of the sea, who will heal all our diseases, and will bear us back upon his own shoulders to the place of honor which originally was ours.

Bernard of Clairvaux[6]

The Lord of the universe has
prevented us, visited us, assisted us;
that sovereign majesty has willed to die
that we might live,
willed to serve
that we might reign,
willed to suffer exile
that we might be brought home,
willed to stoop to the meanest services
that he might set us over the works of his hands.

Bernard of Clairvaux[7]

*We who were made in the form of God but
have been deformed by sin can 'return and be
converted to the Word to be reformed by him
and conformed to him'.[8] 'Who would not be
amazed at the love of God in recalling someone
who has spurned him?'[9] —and yet God does
just that, over and over again.*

God has the words of eternal life, and the hour is coming
—if only it were already here!—when the dead shall hear
his voice, and those who hear him shall live, for life is
in his will. And if you want to know, his will is our
conversion. Listen to him then: 'Is it my will that the
wicked shall die', says the Lord 'and not instead that
he should be converted and live?' From these words we
realize that there is no true life except in conversion and
that there is no other means of entering into life, as the
Lord likewise says: 'Unless you are converted and become as little children, you shall not enter the kingdom
of heaven'.

Bernard of Clairvaux[10]

*This conversion, this turning around or turning
back to our true selves and to God, comes about
when we*

. . . return to our hearts, for this is where he who calls
transgressors back with such anxious solicitude shows
us his salvation.

Bernard of Clairvaux[11]

Only when we return to our hearts and look honestly at ourselves can we begin to recognize ourselves, as we were created to be and as we are. Only then can we learn to know and love ourselves, and to love others as we love ourselves.

Begin to recognize yourself, to love and possess yourself, to be kind to yourself, and you will be happy. If you desire to know yourself and to possess yourself, go into yourself, and do not search for yourself outside. Distinguish between what is around you, what belongs to you, and your self! The world surrounds you, your body belongs to you, and you yourself are within, made to the image and likeness of God. Return then, transgressor, to your heart, within, where you are truly yourself. Outwardly you are an animal, fashioned as the world is fashioned, and that is why man is called a miniature world. But inwardly you are made in the image of God and so are capable of being deified.

Now when a person comes to himself as did that young prodigal son, where does he find himself? Is it not in a far country, in the Land of Unlikeness, and in a strange land, where he sits down and weeps as he remembers his father and his home. And does he not find cause for sorrow in himself, feeding pigs while he himself is starving? If the many hired men in his father's house have bread enough and to spare, while he, the son, in exile and dire poverty, cannot find even husks with which to fill his stomach, will not his tears flow readily enough?

O Adam, where are you? Still in the shadows perhaps, so that you cannot see yourself? Sewing silly fig leaves together to cover your shame? Your eyes are only too open to what is around you and what belongs to you. But look within, see yourself; there you will find things which are much more shameful than those external things of which you are so ashamed. Turn inward, sinner, to your soul. Look at it dominated by vanity and ill-will, so fettered that it cannot break loose; and mourn for it.

We may say that one has only to probe the depths of his own wretchedness, ignorance, neediness and unbridled passions and make an honest reckoning with his conscience, and he will mourn, weep and lament more deeply for himself than at the funeral of anyone else, however dear. His own plight is so much the closer to him as it is within him. Why have sympathy for others, but none for yourself?

Isaac of Stella[12]

The first step for the wretched person extricating himself from the depths of vice is the mercy which makes him merciful to the son of his mother, to be merciful to his soul, and thereby pleasing to God. In this way he emulates the great work of divine pity, being moved to tears with him who was pierced for him, somehow dying for his own salvation, and sparing himself no longer. The first act of pity sustains the person returning to his heart, and enables him to enter the secret places of his being. It now remains for him to link up with the royal road and go forward to truth, and join confession of the lips to contrition of heart, as I have so often urged you to do. For one believes with his heart and so is justified, and he confesses with his lips and so is saved. Turned back to his heart, he must become little in his own

eyes, as Truth himself has said, 'Unless you turn back
and become like little children, you will never enter the
kingdom of heaven'. May he not choose to hide what he
knows only too well, that he is reduced to nothing. May
he not be ashamed to bring into the light of truth what
he cannot see in secret without being moved to pity. In
this way one enters the ways of mercy and truth, the
ways of the Lord, the ways of life.

Bernard of Clairvaux[13]

In this turning back to God, there is a paradox:

Let the soul harken to the divine voice, and to her own
amazement and wonder she will hear it say, 'Blessed are
the poor in spirit, for theirs is the kingdom of heaven'.
Who is poorer in spirit than the person whose spirit
finds no rest and who has nowhere to lay his head?
This also is a counsel of devotion, that the one who is
displeasing to himself is pleasing to God, and one who
hates his own house, that is to say a house full of filth and
wretchedness, is invited to the house of glory, a house not
made with hands, eternal in the heavens. It is no wonder
if such a one trembles with awe at the greatness of this
honor, and finds it hard to believe what he has heard, if
he starts in astonishment and says, 'Is it possible for such
wretchedness to make a man happy?'

Whoever you are, if you are in this frame of mind, do
not despair: it is mercy, not misery, that can make you
happy, but mercy's natural home is misery. Indeed it
happens that misery becomes the source of man's happiness when humiliation turns into humility and necessity

becomes a virtue. As it is written, 'Rain in abundance,
O God, you shed abroad; you restored your heritage as it
languished'. Sickness has real utility when it leads us to
the doctor's hands, and he whom God restores to health
gains by having been ill.

Bernard of Clairvaux[14]

*Moreover, in this paradoxical lesson, God en-
courages us by asking us reassuringly:*

Shall I, who pursue you when you flee from me, reject
you when you come to me? Shall I, who embrace and
draw you to myself when you turn your face from me,
push you away when you hide under the wings of my
mercy?

Aelred of Rievaulx[15]

There is many a consolation to relieve the torment of
a guilty conscience. God is kind and does not let us be
tempted beyond our strength. Especially at the beginning of our conversion, he anoints our wounds with the
oil of mercy so that the acute nature of our sickness and
the difficulty of the cure are perceived only to the extent
that is expedient. On us seems to smile a sort of easi-
ness, which later disappears when the senses have been
trained by practice to fight, so that one may overcome
and come to learn that wisdom is more powerful than
anything.

Bernard of Clairvaux[16]

Just as John [the Baptist] came before Jesus, so penance comes before grace, before that grace of reconciliation which receives us into the kiss of peace after we have made satisfaction. For in this way of penance righteousness and peace kiss each other and run with eager and lighthearted step to meet him. The righteousness, that is, of the person who does penance and the peace of God who forgives; both celebrate with a holy kiss the happy and joyful pact of reconciliation.

Guerric of Igny[17]

'Prepare the way of the Lord', [Saint John the Baptist] says, 'make straight his paths'. One prepares the way who amends his life; one makes straight the path who directs his footsteps along the narrow way. An amended life is certainly the straight road by which the Lord, who in this very conversion is already there before us, may come to us. For indeed it is by the Lord that the steps of a man are directed, and he wants the road to be such that coming along it joyfully towards man he may continually walk with him. For unless he who is the Life, the Truth and the Way anticipates his own coming to us, our way cannot be corrected according to the model of truth, and so cannot be directed to the way of eternity. By what does a youth correct his way, if not by observing his words, if not by following in the footsteps of him who made himself the Way by which we might come to him? O that my ways may be directed to keeping your ways, O Lord, so that because of the words from your lips I may follow even difficult ways. And if they should seem hard to the flesh that is weak they will seem sweet and pleasant to the spirit if it is resolute. 'His ways are pleasant ways and all his paths make for peace'. says the inspired writer. The ways of Wisdom are not only at peace, they bring peace.

Guerric of Igny[18]

Wisdom not only came into the world, but comes into each soul which turns back to God, for turning is already in itself the work of love:

I will flee from the sight of the anger of the Lord and go to a place of refuge, to that zeal of mercy which burns sweetly and wholly purifies. Does not love make amends? Truly it does powerfully. I have read that it covers a multitude of sins. But I would ask this: is it not right and sufficient to cast down and humble all pride of eyes and heart? Yes indeed, for love does not vaunt itself and is not puffed up. Therefore if Our Lord Jesus condescends to come to me, or rather enter into me, not in the zeal of anger or even in wrath, but in love and in a spirit of gentleness, striving with me with the striving of God—for what greater attribute of God is there than love?—then he is indeed God. If he comes in such a spirit, then I know that he is not alone but that the Father is with him. What could be more like a father? Therefore he is not only called the Father of the Word, but the Father of mercies, because it is his nature always to have mercy and to pardon.

Bernard of Clairvaux[19]

Take from me, O Lord, my heart of stone.
Take away my hardened heart.
Take away my uncircumcised heart.
Give me a new heart, a heart of flesh, a pure heart!
You who purify the heart,
you who love the pure heart,
possess my heart and dwell within it,
enclosing it and filling it,
higher than what in me is highest, more
inward than my most inward part.
O form of beauty and seal of sanctity,
seal my heart in your image,
seal my heart under your mercy,
O God of my heart,
O God my portion for ever.

Baldwin of Forde[20]

*The soul that begins the journey back to God
realizes that even this new beginning is a gift
from God, and exclaims in exultation:*

'I found him,' the soul says, 'I found him', though previously he sought and found me like a stray sheep, like a lost coin, and in his mercy anticipated me. He forestalled me, I say, in finding me when I was lost. He anticipated me, though I deserved nothing. He found me astray, he anticipated me in my despair. He found me in my unlikeness; he anticipated me in my diffidence. He found me by pointing out my state to me, he anticipated me by recalling me to his own. He found me wandering in a labyrinth; he anticipated me with gifts when I was devoid of grace. He found me not that I might choose him but that he might choose me. He anticipated me that he might love me before I loved him.

In this way, then, chosen and loved, sought and acquired, found and anticipated, how should I not love and seek him with an effort according to my strength and with affection beyond my strength? I will seek him until gaining my desire I may utter my cry of happiness: 'I have found him whom my soul loves'.

Gilbert of Hoyland[21]

O God, love, who have created me,
recreate me in your love.
O love, who have redeemed me,
whatever I have neglected of your love,
amend for yourself and redeem in me.
O God, love, who with the blood of your
Christ have ransomed me for yourself,
sanctify me in your truth.
O God, love, who have adopted me as your child,
nourish, nourish me after your own heart.
O love, who have chosen me for
yourself and for no one else,
make me, all of me, cling to you.
O God, love, who have cherished me gratuitously,
grant that I may cherish you
with all my heart, all my soul, all my strength.

Gertrud of Helfta[22]

And to the soul that cries out, God replies, encouraging her to continue and to intensify her lessons in love:

Even now you have a partial likeness, because you know partially. 'With face unveiled' you are 'already contemplating my glory', but yet you are still 'being transformed from one degree of glory to another'. While you are being transformed, you do not yet possess wholly. To be transformed is to make progress, but not yet to have been made perfect.

Your perfection, however, is not yet yours, but already my eyes see it; with me you already are such as you will be, O bride. Already you have been written in the book of life and I have your portrait in my hands. Your face is before me always; it shines bright before me, though in you at present it is obscured. Already I have found the drachma of my image in you, but it is still coated with rust and its beauty is hidden. Faith already glows on your cheeks and suffuses them with the color of life, but the object of faith is in hiding.

Gilbert of Hoyland[23]

O love, most almighty God, embolden me in your love.
O wisest love, grant that I may love you wisely.
O most sweet love, grant that I may taste you pleasantly.
O dearest love, grant that I may live for you alone.
O most faithful love, console and
aid me in every tribulation.
O most companionable love, work all my works in me.
O most victorious love, grant that I
may persevere in you to the very end.
O love very close to my heart, who have never
forsaken me, to you I commend my spirit.

Gertrud of Helfta[24]

Sources and Scriptural References

1. *On The Song of Songs* 82.2: CF 40:172–173.
2. *Exposition on the Song of Songs* 83; CF 6:69.
   Gn 1:26; Ps 18:10; Jn 1:14.
3. *On Grace and Free Choice* 10.32–3; CF 19:88–89.
   Lk 15:8; Si 45:2; Phil 2:6.
4. First Sermon for Advent; translation forthcoming in CF 51.
5. Sermon 7.5; CF 14:112.
   Ps 45:8; Lk 10:30–34; Heb 7:19; Rom 3:20; Heb 9:14.
6. Third Sermon for Christmas Eve 1; translation forthcoming in CF 51.
   Mi 7:19; Ps 103:3; Lk 15:5.
7. Third Sermon for Ascension; translation forthcoming in CF 52.
   Ps 8:7.
8. Bernard of Clairvaux, *On the Song of Songs* 83.2; CF 40:182.
   Sg 7:10.
9. Bernard of Clairvaux, *On the Song of Songs* 82.8; CF 40:179.
10. *On Conversion* 1; CF 25:31.
    Jn 6:69; Jn 5:25; Ps 30:5; Mt 11:14; Ez 18:23; 1 Tm 6:19; Mt 18:3.
11. *On Conversion* 7; CF 25:39.
    Is 46:8.
12. Sermon 2.11–15; CF 11:14–15.
    Gn 1:26; Is 46:8; Lk 15:17; Ps 136:4; Gn 3:9.
13. *Sermons on Psalm 90* 11.9; CF 25:209–210.
    Lk 1:79; Is 49:5; Si 30:24; Is 46:8; Nm 21:22; Rom 10:10; Ps 84:8; Mt 18:3; Ps 73:21; Ps 16:11.
14. *On Conversion* 12; CF 25:45–46.
    Mt 5:3; Lk 11:24; Mt 9:20; 1 Cor 7:32; 2 Cor 5:1; Rom 10:16; Ps 68:9.
15. *The Mirror of Charity* 2.11.17; CF 17:181.
16. *On Conversion* 7; CF 25:40.
    1 Cor 10:13; Heb 5:14; Wis 10:12.
17. Sermon 5,2; CF 8:32.
    Ps 85:11.
18. Sermon 4.2; CF 8:24–5.
    Mk 1:3; Ps 37:23; Jn 14:6; Ps 119:9,5; Prv 16:7.

19. *On the Song of Songs* 69.6; CF 40:32–33.
    Jer 4:26; 1 Pt 4:8; Si 23:5; 1 Cor 13:4; 1 Cor 4:21; Jn 4:16; Jn
    16:32; 2 Cor 1:3.
20. Tractate 10/1; CF 41:83.
    Ez 11:19; Ps 72:26.
21. Sermon 8.8; CF 14:125.
    Sg 3:4; Mt 18:12; Lk 15:9; Ps 58:11.
22. Spritual Exercise 5; CF 49:91–92.
    Acts 20:28; Jn 17:17.
23. Sermon 25.4; CF 20:309–310.
    1 Cor 13:9; 2 Cor 3:18.
24. Spritual Exercise 5; CF 49:92.
    Is 26:12; Lk 25:46; Ps 31:6.

4 ∾

Seeking God

Once we have begun to return to God and to our true selves, the Cistercians advise us to 'make our own the humble art of ascending to heaven'.[1] One of their favorite ways to describe this process of transformation is 'seeking God'.

*T*O SEEK GOD is a great good; in my opinion the soul knows no greater blessing. It is the first of her gifts and the final stage in her progress. It is inferior to none, and it yields place to none. What could be superior to it, when nothing has a higher place? What could claim a higher place, when it is the consummation of all things? What virtue can be attributed to anyone who does not seek God? What boundary can be set for anyone who does seek him? The psalmist says: 'Seek his face always'.

Bernard of Clairvaux[2]

'To seek the face of God' is to seek knowledge of him face to face, as Jacob saw him. It is of this knowledge the Apostle says: 'Then I shall know as I am known; now we see a confused reflection in a mirror, but then we shall see face to face; we shall see him as he is'. Always to seek God's face in this life by keeping the hands unstained and the heart clean is that piety which, as Job says, 'is the worship of God'. The one who lacks it 'has received his soul in vain', that is to say, lives to no purpose or does not live at all, since he does not live the life for which he received his soul. This piety is the continual remembrance of God, an unceasing effort of the mind to know him, an unwearied concern of the affections to love him.

William of Saint Thierry[3]

Our search is conducted with the help of Christ, who is both the source and the goal of our seeking.

When Christ says; 'I am the Way and the Truth', he adds, 'and the Life'. It is as if he said: 'I am the Way, I lead to Truth; I am the Truth, I promise Life; and I myself am the very Life I give you'. There are some who go astray and cannot find the road. He cries to them: 'I am the Way'. Some doubt and waver in their faith. His word to them is: 'I am the Truth'. To those who grow weary with the climbing his cry is: 'I am the Life'.

Bernard of Clairvaux[4]

He who is the Way, the Truth and the Life corrects, guides and welcomes.

Isaac of Stella[5]

We are encouraged in the search, because if the Lord is so good to the soul who seeks him, what must he be to the one who finds him?

Bernard of Clairvaux[6]

> As we seek God, we acknowledge our weak-
> ness, our waywardness, our helplessness, and
> we trust in his goodness, mercy, and faithful-
> ness.

Lord my God, I know, in the light of your revelation, how much I lack in perfection and knowledge, and this I reckon no little wisdom here on earth, I think this no little step on the way to perfection, to know how far I am removed from wisdom and far removed from the paths of the perfect I am walking. So then, if I am ignorant of anything, provided only that I know I am ignorant, then, as the Wise Man says, 'my ignorance will remain with me', and my weakness will be a great help and support to me, again provided that I keep it before my eyes. This twofold knowledge of my wretchedness shines like light in darkness, making me gleam with brightness in your presence, Lord my God, and preparing me, I hope, to gaze upon your countenance. Certainly, the surest preparation for knowing you is to have known myself fully.

John of Forde[7]

I will love you, good Jesus. I will love you, my Strength, whom I cannot love without your help and cannot love as you deserve. May my endeavors be directed to you without reserve and may they not be diverted and distracted by any other affection. But even when totally directed toward you, how feeble are our endeavors! How then shall I weaken what is so feeble even at full strength? May I be wholly carried to you by my desires, good God. Draw me to yourself that I may require no stimulus of fear and that perfect charity may banish any recourse to fear.

Gilbert of Hoyland[8]

We seek by means of faith, hope and love.

In God we live through faith, we move and advance through hope, we have our being, that is, our fixed dwelling-place through love.

William of Saint Thierry[9]

Faith lengthens the soul, charity widens it, hope gives it height.

Isaac of Stella[10]

We are led back from our deformity to our true form by these three: faith, hope, and love, so that we may know what we must believe, in what we must hope, what we must love.

Aelred of Rievaulx[11]

O you whom no one truly seeks and does not find,
come within us
that we may go to you and live in you,
for surely this comes not from the person
willing, nor from the person running
but from you who have mercy!
Inspire us first that we may believe!
Strengthen us that we may hope!
Call us forth and set us on fire that we may love.
May everything of ours be yours,
that we may truly be in you,
in whom we live and move and have our being.

William of Saint Thierry[12]

*Our first means of seeking is faith. Faith relies
on what we cannot see; yet by faith we not only
seek, but also find, God.*

Come then, follow, seek him; do not let that unapproachable brightness and glory hold you back from seeking
him or make you despair of finding him. 'If you can
believe, all things are possible to him who believes'.

'The Word is near you, in your mouth and in your heart'.
Believe, and you have found him. Believing is having
found. The faithful know that Christ dwells in their
hearts by faith. What could be nearer? Therefore seek
him confidently, seek him faithfully. 'The Lord is good
to the soul who seeks him'. Seek him in your prayers,
follow him in your actions, find him in faith. How can
faith fail to find him? It reaches what is unreachable,
makes known what is unknown, grasps what cannot be

measured, plumbs the uttermost depths, and in a way encompasses even eternity itself in its wide embrace.

Bernard of Clairvaux[13]

The fact that faith is shadowy is a blessing; it tempers the light to the eye's weakness and prepares the eye for the light, for it is written: 'He cleansed their hearts by faith'. Faith therefore does not quench the light but protects it. If you cannot yet grasp the naked truth is it not worthwhile to possess it wrapped in a veil?

Bernard of Clairvaux[14]

The virtue of faith, contemplating not what is visible but what is invisible, is twofold, just as the concept of things invisible is twofold. Things are not seen either because they are not present, or because even though present they are spiritual entities. The good things to come that have been promised are not yet present. God himself, he who promises or threatens, is present, but owing to his spiritual nature he lies hidden. Now because faith is the substance of things to be hoped for it lays hold of the good things to come that are the object of its hope as if they were already present, and makes them as it were already exist in the heart of the believer. In the same way, because it is the evidence of things that appear not, it exposes, examines and demonstrates to itself the presence of God, even though he appears not. To him who said: 'He it is who has raised us up together and has made us sit together in the heavenly places through Christ Jesus', faith was indeed the substance of things to be hoped for. To him who endured as seeing him that is invisible, faith was the evidence of things that appear not. For the one who said: 'We are saved by hope', did he not clearly show that through faith the object of his hope and enduring expectation already abode in his heart? And is not the one who holds God constantly in his sight persuaded by the evidence of faith that he is present even though he appears not?

To this kind of faith the words of Scripture are directly applicable: 'The just person lives by faith'. For this is the faith which makes him just and keeps him just and, so that he may live for ever, feeds him in the meantime with the joy of hope. For what can recall a person from the path of sin and save him so well as the faith which endures and preserves, seeing him that is invisible? What makes a person rejoice with hope so well as the faith which always looks to the reward?

Guerric of Igny[15]

*Our faith leads us to hope. We place our hope,
our trust, in God alone.*

Hope stands firm in the refusal to put no trust at all in its own wisdom and power. But this makes it cleave all the more wisely and strongly to God's wisdom and power. If it thinks it can do nothing without God, it is just as convinced that in him it can do everything.

O how lovingly we can expect everything from God, when we expect nothing from ourselves! There is nothing I cannot do in him, knowing as I do that there is nothing I can do without him.

John of Forde[16]

How much better, how much safer, it is to have him caring for me than to be looking after myself. Indeed, I am poor and needy, but if the Lord takes thought for me I am rich and blessed; no mistake, everything works for good in me. Therefore let those who know your name put their trust in you, for you, O Lord, do not forsake them.

Guerric of Igny[17]

How glad I should be, Lord, Jesus, to glory—if I could—in my infirmity, that your virtue, your humility, might be made perfect in me. When my own virtue fails, your grace is sufficient for me.

Bernard of Clairvaux[18]

Faith and hope lead in turn naturally to love.

Anyone who truly believes in God and hopes in him and knows him cannot fail to love him.

William of Saint Thierry[19]

We must persevere in the school of love if we are to continue learning God's ways and being formed by and to them. Above all, we must pray to the Lord to lead us into the school of love where we may learn further to recognize and love Jesus.

If only you would now open to me the school of chaste cherishing-love that therein I might experience your dearest discipline and through you be allotted a soul not only good but, in truth, both holy and perfect.

O love, dip my senses in the marrow of your charity so that through you I may become a gifted child and you yourself may be, in truth, my Father, teacher, and master. And under your fatherly blessing, let my spirit be wholly purified and refined.

O God, love, if you now unfolded your wondrous alphabet to me that my heart might enroll itself in the same curriculum as you! Tell me now by living experience what the glorious and foremost *alpha* of your beautiful cherishing-love is like; and do not conceal from me that fruitful *beta* which fills generations with your imperial wisdom. Diligently and one by one, show me with the finger of your Spirit the individual letters of your charity. Then reaching the very marrow of the foretaste of your gentleness, let me, in truth, with the clean eye of my heart, scrutinize and examine, learn more, know and recognize them as wholly was is lawful in this life.

Teach me through the co-operation of your Spirit the *tau* of supreme perfection and lead me to the *omega* of full consummation. In this life make me so perfectly learn more of your scripture, which is full of charity and cherishing-love, that in fulfilling your charity not one *iota* in me may be idle.

Gertrud of Helfta[20]

Sources and Scriptural References

1. *The Golden Epistle* 8; CF 12:10.
2. *On the Song of Songs* 84.1; CF 40:188.
   Sg 3:1; Ps 105:4.
3. *The Golden Epistle* 26-27; CF 12:18.
   Ps 24:4; Gn 32:30; 1 Cor 13:12; 1 Jn 3:2.
4. *The Steps of Humility* 1; CF 13:29-30.
   Jn 14:6.
5. Sermon 1.17; CF 11:7.
6. *On Loving God* 22; CF 13:114-115.
   Lam 3:25.
7. Sermon 108.5; CF 47:96.
   Jb 19:4.
8. Sermon 19.6; CF 20:245.
   Ps 18:1; 1 Jn 4:18.
9. *The Golden Epistle* 207; CF 12:81.
   Acts 17:28.
10. Sermon 8.4; CF 11:66.
11. Sermons on Isaiah 2. The english translation has been delayed in anticipation of a critical latin edition.
12. *The Mirror of Faith* 32; CF 15:86.
    Mt 7:7; Rom 9:16; Acts 17:28.
13. *On the Song of Songs* 76.6; CF 40:114-115.
    1 Tm 6:10; Mk 9:22; Rom 10:8.
14. *On the Song of Songs* 31.9; CF 7:132.
    Acts 15:9.
15. Sermon 25.3-4; CF 32:27-28.
    Heb 11:1; Eph 2:6; Heb 11:27; Rom 8:24; Ps 16:8; Rom 1:17.
16. Sermon 65.6; CF 45:40-41.
    Jn 15:5; Phil 4:13.
17. Sermon 23.3; CF 32:12.
    Ps 70:6; Ps 40:18; Rom 8:28; Ps 9:11.
18. *The Steps of Humility* 26; CF 13:54-55.
    2 Cor 12:7-8.
19. *Exposition on the Song of Songs* 28; CF 6:22.
20. Spiritual Exercise 5; CF 49:84-85.
    Ws 8:19; Lk 11:20; Rv 1:8.

5 ❧

Learning to Love

Faith and hope lead us to want to have what we believe in and hope for. The more we want it, the more we learn to love it and want to concentrate on it. Our turning back to God is made easier if we take practical steps, which include turning away from other things which attract and distract us and going apart in solitude, being still so that we can listen to God.

S EE HOW HIDDENLY Christ prays, Christ who taught us to pray in secret to the Father. You too, make for yourself a hidden place within yourself, in which you can flee away from yourself and pray in secret to the Father.

Isaac of Stella[1]

And now, Desire of my soul,
my soul desires to wait on you a little space,
and to taste and see how gracious you are, O Lord.
I implore your tender mercy
to give me peace and silence from all things,
whether outward or inward.

William of Saint Thierry[2]

If you ask me how to obtain the delights of contemplation, my immediate answer is by living in the wilderness
and coming up from it. You know what scripture says:
'The Lord God will make the wilderness of Sion like
delights, and her desert like the garden of the Lord'.
Stay in solitude and be silent; deep within your own self
make a pleasant and blooming solitude; wait in silence
for God's salvation, and if he keeps you waiting for a little
while, do not lose patience but go on patiently waiting.
In fact, the One we wait for is attentively watchful of a
person who can say: 'I waited patiently for the Lord'. He
says: it is patiently I have waited, meaning that I have
persevered in my waiting; I have trusted him, and so my
waiting will never meet with disappointment.

Yes indeed, Jeremiah bears witness that it is good to
wait patiently for the Lord, and it is a work of great
virtue to be wholly dependent on the return of Jesus.
During this waiting, the soul is strengthened and it
purifies its spirit; it thinks everything that could impede
the returning footsteps of its spouse, is to be mistrusted.
So waiting is good when it prepares the way for the
spouse, makes him come more quickly, a waiting that
girds up loins and lights up lamps and makes ready the
marriage bed.

Yes, a good time of waiting, making one come up from
the wilderness, or, in other words, making one penetrate
the profound secrets of the depths of solitude through
daily progress in virtue. What could be more secret
than this solitude? The nobler it is, the sweeter and
more delightful, as the song proclaims: 'Who is this', say
the daughters, 'coming up from the wilderness, flowing
with delights?' We shall enjoy that flowing pleasure all

the more when we have worked patience and grown holier by waiting.

John of Forde[3]

Christ the Lord is a spirit before your face, and he demands solitude of the spirit more than of the body, although physical withdrawal can be of benefit when the opportunity offers, especially in time of prayer. To do this is to follow the advice and example of the bridegroom, shut the door and then pray. And what he said he did. He spent nights alone in prayer, not merely hiding from the crowds but even from his disciples and familiar friends. He did indeed take three of his friends with him when the hour of his death was approaching; but the urge to pray drew him apart even from them. You too must act like this when you wish to pray.

Apart from that the only solitude prescribed for you is that of the mind and spirit. You enjoy this solitude if you refuse to share in the common gossip, if you shun involvement in the problems of the hour and set no store by the fancies that attract the masses; if you reject what everybody covets, avoid disputes, make light of losses, and pay no heed to injuries. Otherwise you are not alone even when alone. Do you not see that you can be alone when in company and in company when alone? However great the crowds that surround you, you can enjoy the benefits of solitude if you refrain from curiosity about other people's conduct and shun rash judgment.

Bernard of Clairvaux[4]

Anyone who wishes to pray must choose not only the right place but also the right time. A time of leisure is

best and most convenient, the deep silence when others
are asleep is particularly suitable, for prayer will then
be freer and purer. 'Arise at the first watch of the night,
and pour out your heart like water before the face of
the Lord, your God'. How secretly prayer goes up in the
night, witnessed only by God and the holy angel who
received it to present it at the heavenly altar!

Bernard of Clairvaux[5]

Give me, O Lord,
the comfort of my wilderness:
a solitary heart and frequent communing with you.
As long as you are with me, O my God,
I shall not be alone;
but if you leave me, woe to him that is alone;
for if I fall asleep,
there will be no one to keep me warm;
if I fall down,
there will be nobody to pick me up.

William of Saint Thierry[6]

If you have fled away to remain in solitude, continue to
stay there; wait there for the One who will save you 'from
pusillanimity of spirit and the storm'. However much
the storm of battles may assail you, however much you
may feel the lack even of sustenance in the desert, do
not because of pusillanimity of spirit return in mind to
Egypt. The desert will feed you more abundantly with
manna, that is, the bread of angels, than Egypt with its
fleshpots. Jesus himself fasted indeed in the wilderness
but the multitude that followed him into the desert he
fed often and in a wonderful manner. And much more

frequently and in an even more wonderful way will he satisfy the needs of you who have followed him into the desert.

Guerric of Igny[7]

In learning to listen and to love, more important even than exterior solitude is interior silence. The Word of God became human to speak to us and to give us an example of silent attentiveness. And he continues to speak, if only we are silent enough to hear him.

If in the depths of your soul you were to keep a quiet silence, the all-powerful Word would flow from the Father's throne secretly into you. Happy then is the person who has so fled the world's tumult, who has so withdrawn into the solitude and secrecy of interior peace, that he can hear not only the Voice of the Word, but the Word himself: not John but Jesus.

Guerric of Igny[8]

The silence of the Word in the womb of the virgin speaks to you, cries out to you, recommends the discipline of silence. For 'in silence and in hope shall be your strength' as Isaiah promises, who defined the pursuit of justice as silence. As the Christ-child in the womb advanced towards birth in a long, deep silence, so does the discipline of silence nourish, form and strengthen a person's spirit, and produce growth which is the safer and more wholesome for being the more hidden.

Guerric of Igny[9]

Truly a trustworthy word and deserving of every welcome, O Lord, is your almighty Word, which in so deep a
silence made its way down from the Father's royal throne
into the mangers of animals and meanwhile speaks to
us better by its silence. Let him who has ears to hear,
hear what this loving and mysterious silence of the eternal Word speaks to us. For, unless hearing deceives me,
among the other things which he speaks, he speaks
peace for the holy people upon whom reverence for him
and his example impose a religious silence. And most
rightly was it imposed. For what recommends the discipline of silence with such weight and such authority,
what checks the evil of restless tongues and the storms
of words, as the Word of God silent in our midst? I
would gladly be dumb and be brought low, and be silent
even from good things, that I might be able the more
attentively and diligently to apply my ear to the secret
utterances and sacred meaning of this divine silence,
learning in silence in the school of the Word.

Guerric of Igny[10]

*By leisurely, attentive, meditative reading,
called* lectio *by Cistercians and others who follow the Rule, we gradually learn to know and
to love God , taught by those who have done so
before us.*

Haphazard reading, constantly varied and as if lighted
upon by chance does not edify but makes the mind un-
stable; taken into the memory lightly, it goes out from it
even more lightly. But you should concentrate on certain
authors and let your mind grow accustomed to them.

Reading should also stimulate the feelings and give rise to prayer, which should interrupt your reading: an interruption which should not so much hamper the reading as restore to it a mind ever more purified for understanding.

For reading serves the purpose of the intention with which it is done. If the reader truly seeks God in his reading, everything that he reads tends to promote that end, making the mind surrender in the course of the reading and bring all that is understood into Christ's service.

William of Saint Thierry[11]

Reading should serve prayer, should dispose the affections, should neither devour the hours nor gobble up the moments of prayer. When you read you are taught about Christ, but when you pray you join him in familiar colloquy. How much more enchanting is the grace of speaking with him than about him!

Gilbert of Hoyland[12]

The light of wisdom is kindled by fervent prayer, just as the light of knowledge is by frequent reading, provided that when you read you use a burning lamp, that is, justice in your deeds and devotion in your sentiments.

Guerric of Igny[13]

The very best and most helpful book for meditative reading is Holy Scripture, the written word of the Word of God.

Anyone who thirsts for God eagerly studies and med-
itates on the inspired word, knowing that there he is
certain to find the one for whom he thirsts.

Bernard of Clairvaux[14]

The Scriptures need to be read and understood in the
same spirit in which they were written. You will never
enter into Paul's meaning until by constant application
to reading him and by giving yourself to constant meditation you have imbibed his spirit. You will never understand David until by experience you have made the very
sentiments of the psalms your own. And that applies to
all Scripture. There is the same gulf between attentive
study and mere reading as there is between friendship
and acquaintance with a passing guest, between boon
companionship and chance meeting.

William of Saint Thierry[15]

Search the Scriptures. For you are not mistaken in thinking that you find life in them, you who seek nothing else
in them but Christ, to whom the Scriptures bear witness.
Blessed indeed are they who search his testimonies, seek
them out with all their heart. Your testimonies are wonderful, Lord, therefore my soul has searched them. There
is need for searching not only in order to draw out the
mystical sense but also to taste the moral sense. Therefore
you who walk about in the gardens of the Scriptures do
not pass by heedlessly and idly, but searching each and
every word like busy bees gathering honey from flowers,
reap the Spirit from the words. 'For my Spirit', says Jesus,
'is sweeter than honey and my inheritance surpasses

the honeycomb'. So, proving by experience that hidden manna is savory, you will break forth into those words of David: 'How sweet to my mouth are your words, sweeter than honey and the honeycomb to my palate'.

From these gardens the Bridegroom will lead you, if I be not mistaken, into others where rest is more hidden and enjoyment more blessed and beauty more wonderful. When you are absorbed in his praises with accents of exultation and thanksgiving, he will take you into his wonderful tenting place, into the very house of God, into the unapproachable light in which he dwells, where he feeds, where he lies down at midday. For if the devotion of those who sing psalms or pray has something of that loving curiosity of the disciples who asked: 'Rabbi, where do you dwell?' they deserve, I think, to hear: 'Come and see'. 'They went', we read, and saw and stayed with him that day'.

Guerric of Igny[16]

By reading and pondering the Scriptures, we learn to know Christ, who speaks to us through them. Christ is both our teacher and the lesson we learn.

The soul at prayer should have before her a sacred image of the God-man, in his birth or infancy or as he was teaching, or dying, or rising, or ascending. Whatever form it takes this image must bind the soul with the love of virtue and expel carnal vices, eliminate temptations and quiet desires.

Bernard of Clairvaux[17]

Let this man Christ be your one teacher, this man who is, for your sake, a scroll written on the inside of the page and on the outside. Read of this man by reading him, learn from him by learning him. Copy from this pattern the pattern both on the inside and on the outside of yourselves, in your interior and in your behavior. Your lives should teach others to live as he lived. This is why we are told: 'Glorify and carry God about in your bodies'. May he himself make us this very gift. Amen.

Isaac of Stella[18]

Conversion, silence, solitude, reading, and med-itation are all meant to lead us to prayer. The early Cistercians learned their lesson well and have bequeathed us many insights about praying.

Prayer is the affection of a person who clings to God, a certain familiar and devout conversation, a state in which the enlightened mind enjoys God as long as it is permitted. 'Pray without interruption and give thanks at all times'. This prayer is a certain unchanging goodness of the mind and of the well-ordered spirit and a certain resemblance to the goodness of their Father, God, on the part of God's sons. It prays for everyone always and gives thanks for everything. It continually pours itself out before God in as many kinds of prayer or thanksgiving as its devout affection finds occasion in its needs or con-solations, and also in sharing its neighbor's pains or joys. It is constantly absorbed in thanksgiving because to be in such a state is to be always in the joy of the Holy Spirit.

William of Saint Thierry[19]

You urge me to lay down for you some rule for contemplating the Beloved and to give you a method for this discovery and vision. What does this mean? Would you have me confine within a rule the bounty of God's gift? This vision results not from human effort but from grace. It is the fruit of revelation, not of research. If, however, effort can contribute to this end, observe first the advice of Isaiah: 'Wash, make yourselves clean'. Secondly, write about wisdom in your time of leisure, for one who is relieved of other tasks will acquire wisdom. Thirdly, be violent and capture the joy of the kingdom too long withheld from you.

So you are advised to keep your heart purified, prompt and importunate. By the first you will become worthy, by the second devout, by the third eager; that is, worthy, attentive and insistent: worthy to welcome grace, meeting it on the way, impatient when it delays. By the first you are prepared; by the second you are likened to the bride as she waits for her Beloved to return from the wedding feast; by the third you hasten, just as the bride who does not wait but hastens and bypasses even the watchmen.

Gilbert of Hoyland[20]

If you are to go around the Lord's altar with a clean heart, then do not be slow to wash your hands. When you have clean hands, your prayer springs forth with greater purity and freedom. Its passage is swifter, it penetrates more deeply, it enters God's presence more pleasingly.

John of Forde[21]

Dogged prayer reaches its goal. And if at the beginning prayer seems to you dry and stoney, still from this hardest of rocks you will squeeze the oil of grace if only you persevere, if protracted delay does not sap your strength, if your longings do not grow slack from deferral. Deferral is obviously painful to a lover but desires prolonged grow stronger.

Gilbert of Hoyland[22]

Prayer fulfills the function of both myrrh and incense. First it gathers and binds together into yourself your affections when you pray; then it releases them to transmit them to God. What is more like myrrh, when there is such an outpouring towards union with God? Rightly is the bride called all fair and flawless, when the ardor of prayer makes her incandescent, when the brightness of eternal light dyes her with its color and makes her radiant.

'You are all fair, my love; there is no flaw in you'. 'You are all fair', because you are wholly beautiful, especially at this hour, the hour of prayer, the hour of incense. 'You are all fair my love, you are all fair', because you are wholly beloved and incandescent with the sole affection of love. 'You are all fair and without flaw', having no admixture of alien hue. 'Come from Lebanon; come from Lebanon, come from Lebanon!' 'Come from Lebanon', because you are all fair! 'Come from Lebanon', because you are fully cleansed. 'Come from Lebanon', wholly enlightened; 'come from Lebanon', free from fault; 'come from Lebanon' bright with grace; 'come, you shall wear the crown'.

Utterly happy is one who from the Lebanon of bright affection, from the hill of incense, from abundance of intense prayer, is called to a crown.

Gilbert of Hoyland[23]

Whatever the object of my prayer,
I never pray or worship you in vain;
the very act of praying brings me rich reward.
Teach me then, Holy Spirit, to pray without ceasing,
that you may grant me to rejoice unceasingly in you.

William of Saint Thierry[24]

Lord, you are pitying and merciful, patient and kind beyond all measure. You are gracious to all, and your compassion rests on all your works. You yourself exhort us, Lord, to pray and to watch in prayer; so does your Holy Spirit.

You exhort us and teach us to do so, out of your tenderness and pity and your will to show us mercy. And you have told us to ask boldly in your name, and to believe that we shall receive whatever we have asked, and that those things for which we pray will come to pass.

And yet, in spite of all your exhortation, we are slow to pray; in spite of your bidding we neglect to do it, and we do not believe your promises. Nevertheless, you in your mercy and your great compassion rouse the slothful and the negligent; your patience overlooks our lack of trust. And further, since we neither know how to pray aright, nor have the power to do so, you send your Holy Spirit, that he may help our weakness and intercede for us with groanings that cannot be uttered.

We pray, therefore, because you tell us to do so; we ask with confidence, because we have your promise; and forthwith you run to meet us and answer our prayer, finding in us a ground for your forgiveness, because you have yourself made us forgivable.

William of Saint Thierry[25]

My sweetest Jesus,
revive my listless spirit in you now,
in your death restore to me a life lived for you alone.
Grant me a way of life corresponding
worthily to the price of your blood.
Grant me a spirit that savors you,
senses that sense you,
a soul that understands your will,
virtue that perfects your gracious purpose,
stability that perseveres with you.

Gertrud of Helfta[26]

Sources and Scriptural References

1. Sermon 1.9; CF 11.5.
   Mt 6:6.
2. *Meditation* 4.9; CF 3:115.
   Is 26:9; Ps 34:9.
3. Sermon 100.6; CF 46:221–222.
   Is 51:3; Lam 3:28; Ps 40:11; Ps 119:116; Lam 3:26; Sg 8:5.

4. *On the Song of Songs* 40.4–5; CF 7:202–203.
   Lam 4:20; Mt 6:6; Lk 6:12; Jn 12:36; Mt 26:37; Lk 10:37; 2
   Sm 19:19.
5. *On the Song of Songs* 86.3; CF 40:213–214.
   Lam 2:19.
6. *Meditation* 4.9; CF 3:115.
   Qo 4:10–11.
7. Sermon 4.1; CF 8:22–23.
   Ws 18:14.
8. Sermon 4.2; CF 8:24
9. Sermon 28.5; CF 32:52.
   Is 30:15; Is 32:17.
10. Sermon 10.2; CF 8:63–64.
    1 Tm 1:15; Ws 18:14; Mt 11:15; Ps 85:9; Ps 39:2.
11. *The Golden Epistle* 1.120–124; CF 12:51–52.
12. Sermon 7.2; CF 14:109.
13. Sermon 13.7; CF 8:90.
14. *On the Song of Songs* 23.3; CF 7:28.
15. *The Golden Epistle* 1.120–124; CF 12:1–51.
16. Sermon 54.2–3; CF 32:214–215.
    Jn 5:39; Ps 119:2, 129; Si 24:27; Ps 119:103; Ps 42:5; 1 Tm
    6:16; Sg 1:6; Jn 1:38–39.
17. *On the Song of Songs* 20.6; CF 4:152.
18. Sermon 8.16; CF 11:71.
    Mt 23:10; Rv 5:1; 1 Cor 6:20.
19. *The Golden Epistle* 179–181; CF 12:71.
    1 Th 5:17; 1 Th 1:6.
20. Sermon 7.1; CF 14:108.
    Is 1:16; Si 38:25; Mt 11:12; Lk 12:36; Sg 3:4.
21. Sermon 51.7; CF 44:65.
22. Sermon 6.1; CF 14:98.
    Dt 32:13.
23. Sermon 28.7; CF 20:348.
    Sg 4:6.
24. *Meditation* 4.13; CF 3:117.
    1 Th 5:16–17.
25. *Meditation* 3.1–2; CF 3:110–111.
    Ps 145:8–9; Mt 26:41; Jn 14:13; Ws 11:24; Gal 4:6.
26. Spiritual Exercise 7; CF 49:141.

6 ∾

Aspects of Love

The image and likeness of God, to which we were formed, was, as we have already seen, deformed by sin. The task we face in the school of love is to let that likeness be re-formed in us.

*T*HE WHOLE ATTENTION of those who love God is fixed on improving and adorning the inward self that is made to the image of God, and is renewed day by day. For they are certain that nothing can be more pleasing to God than his own image when restored to its original beauty. Hence all their glory is within, not without; not in the beauty of nature nor in the praises of the crowd, but in the Lord. With Saint Paul they say: 'Our boast is this, the testimony of our conscience'; because the sole judge of their conscience is God, whom alone they desire to please, and pleasing him is their sole, true and highest glory.

Bernard of Clairvaux[1]

If we love and want to please God, we will want to do his will.

To join one's will to the will of God, so that the human will consents to whatever the divine will prescribes, and so that there is no other reason why it wills this thing or another except that it realizes God wills it: this surely is to love God. The will itself is nothing other than love, and good or bad will should not be called anything but good or bad love.

Aelred of Rievaulx[2]

O love,
begin now to exercise your mastery over me,
removing me from myself
for the ministry of your living
charity and cherishing-love, O love:
possessing, sanctifying, and filling my entire spirit.

Gertrud of Helfta[3]

God wills that we become holy; that is, that we be con-formed to Christ, the Image of the unseen God.

Just as the sea is the ultimate source of wells and rivers, so Christ the Lord is the ultimate source of all virtue and knowledge. From him as from a well-head comes the power to be pure in body, diligent in affection and upright in will. From him too come subtlety of intellect, splendor of eloquence, urbanity of bearing; from him, knowledge and words of wisdom. Indeed in him are hidden all the treasures of wisdom and knowledge. Shall

I add still more? Chaste thoughts, just judgments, holy desires—are they not all streams from that one spring?

Bernard of Clairvaux[4]

Christ was made our wisdom in order to teach us prudence, our righteousness to forgive our sins, our holiness through his example of chaste and temperate living, and our redemption through patience in his resolute acceptance of death.

What have you to do with righteousness, if you are ignorant of Christ, who is the righteousness of God. Where, I ask, is true prudence, except in the teaching of Christ? Or true justice, if not from Christ's mercy? Or true temperance, if not in Christ's life? Or true fortitude, if not in Christ's passion? Vainly will anyone strive to acquire the virtues, if he thinks they may be obtained from any source other than the Lord of the virtues, whose teaching is the seed-bed of prudence, whose mercy is the wellspring of justice, whose life is a mirror of temperance, whose death is the badge of fortitude.

Bernard of Clairvaux[5]

Through temperance we are made pure; through prudence we choose the good and reject evil; through justice we love God and our neighbor; through fortitude we persevere in all these goods.

Aelred of Rievaulx[6]

*Love is what urges us to obedience and patience,
and practising these virtues makes us grow in
love.*

The charity of God and obedience are bound each to
each with an unbreakable bond and in no way separated
from each other. The Lord shows us that there cannot
be charity without obedience when he says, 'If anyone
loves me, he will keep my word'; that is to say, he will
observe my commandments, and in observing them, he
will obey me. And he also shows us that there cannot be
obedience without charity when he says: 'He who does
not love me does not keep my words'. If, then, he who
loves obeys, and he who does not love does not obey, it
follows that just as there cannot be charity without obedience, neither can there be obedience without charity.

Baldwin of Forde[7]

The Lord advised and instructed us to put ourselves
under his yoke and his burden, and thus, through obedience and patience, to become his docile creatures, for it is
in these two virtues, obedience and patience, that docil-
ity to God is shown. Obedience carries out the things we
are instructed to do; patience bears the things which God
imposes upon us and which we must endure. Obedience
is not refractory, and patience does not complain. Obedience stands by the commandments; patience remains
steadfast in judgment. Obedience is a yoke which is no
yoke, for it banishes servitude and restores freedom.
Patience is a burden which is no burden, for rather than
loading us down, it lightens us. Through patience, the
things which the impatient find burdensome are light-
ened, for patience is like a spiritual cart in which we can

carry all our burdens with greater ease. All the plumes and feathers on a bird constitute a sort of burden, but yet they raise it up into the heavens, and in just the same way, patience enables us to rise above tribulation and not to be crushed beneath it. All who become gentle under the yoke and burden of Christ find that God is also gentle with them.

Baldwin of Forde[8]

The royal virtue of patience is fittingly joined to charity, which must of necessity be exercised in exercises of patience. Charity [the highest form of love] is only true when at last it has become patient. Of course, human nature being what it is, it is impossible that patience should be found among us without the hammer of tribulation having worked upon it. But equally, charity that has not been tested by patience will be of little value, and patience which has not been shaped by charity will be altogether shapeless and of no value at all.

John of Forde[9]

Patience is the greatest virtue of all. It secures possession of the soul, no matter what damage the power of the persecutor may inflict on the body. It is the good soil that, as Truth bears witness, yields nothing but a good harvest. The Apostle in this connection has the words, 'You need endurance if you are to attain the prize God has promised to those who do his will'. As the blessed James says, 'It brings to full achievement'. It has two sides that make the mind it possesses both cool and courageous in both prosperity and adversity, be it against the seductive suggestions of the flesh and the swarms of interior vices or against the softness and fierceness of the world outside. May he generously confer such virtue on us, that we may suffer with and for him who suffered with such patience for our sake, Christ Jesus, who with God the Father and the Holy Spirit lives and rules as God for ever and ever.

Isaac of Stella[10]

Love is not an easy lesson to perfect. Even when we have acquired some measure of loving obedience and patience, we still may be aware that

Somewhere in us is still to be found a certain crookedness of will, roughness of character, darkness through lack of understanding and slipperiness through inconsistent behavior. But how will we fulfill what the Scripture says about preparing the way unless we do what is written there, so that the crooked ways may be straight and the rough ways smooth. And so in the first place, if our will is crooked and twisted it must be rectified and corrected to the pattern of the Divine Will. Therefore you who hasten to prepare the way of the Lord, before all else let your will be good, since Wisdom will not enter into a malicious soul.

And when you have thus made the crooked straight, understand that it is no less necessary to make the rough ways plain, that is, to even out harshness of character and diffuse a certain equanimity in your life with others.

And even if you have advanced so far on the way of the Lord, that the road you follow is straight and your life is ordered by gentleness, you have indeed advanced, but you have not yet reached your destination unless the Word of God is a lamp to your feet and a light on your path. The commandment is a lamp, and teaching a light, and the reproofs of discipline the way of life. So if you are wise, you will not be your own teacher and guide in the way along which you have never walked; but you will incline your ear to masters, and acquiesce in their reproofs and advice, and give yourself to the task of learning and *lectio*.

But this way in which we must meet with salvation and the Saviour, just as it is not now darkened through ignorance of the truth, so it should not be slippery from inconstancy in work. Though we see with wide-open eyes because of knowledge, we may fall from negligence. Nor can we make the excuse that the road is slippery; the fault is rather with the intention of the mind, that is, the foot we stand on. For who is not walking in mud while he is in the world, while he is living in his body of clay? It is not so much the road that is at fault as the foot, which is not firmly enough on the way of God.

But the person who falls, shall he not rise again? A righteous person falls seven times a day and rises each time, for the Lord lifts up those who are bowed down and guides the righteous. So when you cannot do otherwise, walk along the road, falling and rising, constantly crying out to him whom you desire to follow and to reach: 'Keep my steps on your paths so that my feet may not slip. And if there is any wicked way in me, that is, any human frailty, lead me in the everlasting way, since it is through you, the Way and the Truth, that I shall come to you, the Life eternal. Glory to you for endless ages'.

Guerric of Igny[11]

Why do we need to learn obedience and patience? Because love, even charity, is a fragile thing and we—and those around us—will fail in its exercise many times over. Gentleness and patience enable us to practice forgiveness.

'Be careful', says the apostle, 'to preserve the unity of the spirit in the bond of peace'. This unity is exceedingly delicate. This is why, very often, when we have some encounter that is less devout or some thought that is less cheerful than we had yesterday or the day before, or when through carelessness, we break out into any indication of having less patience, we are thrown off balance. We are angry and quick tempered, with the result that we learn in our wretchedness how fragile charity is.

If any soul yearns for the transcendent charity of Christ, then her first need is to have this law written in the very center of the heart, for this is the straight and royal road that leads to that royal eminence. In fact, if your heart is agitated with even the smallest dispute over some injury, whether you are enduring it yourself or making another endure it, then there is no room for prayer. No, a cloud presents itself, and lets nothing pass through it. But, on the other hand, if you listen carefully, a voice sounds from the cloud: 'Make peace with your brother or sister', and forgive whatever you have against them.

John of Forde[12]

Our experience of own weakness, even our failures, should not discourage us. God may let us be chastened, but God never abandons us.

Through everything, God is always there, summoning and supporting us.

Expect a twofold help from God in the course of your spiritual life: correction and consolation. One controls the exterior, the other works within; the first curbs arrogance, the latter inspires trust; the first begets humility, the latter strengthens the faint-hearted; the first makes one discreet, the latter devout. The first imbues us with fear of God, the latter tempers that fear with the joy of salvation, as the words of Scripture indicate: 'Let my heart rejoice that it may fear your name'; and 'Serve the Lord with fear, and rejoice before him with reverence'.

Bernard of Clairvaux[13]

A sense of gratitude for God's many blessings will not only lighten our spirits, but will dispose us for still greater gifts.

My advice to you is to turn aside occasionally from troubled and anxious pondering on the paths you may be treading, and to travel on smoother ways where the gifts of God are serenely savored, so that the thought of him may give breathing space to you whose consciences are perplexed. I should like you to experience for yourselves the truth of the holy prophet's words: 'Make the Lord your joy and he will give you what your heart desires'. Sorrow for sin is indeed necessary, but it should not be an endless preoccupation. You must dwell also on the glad remembrance of God's loving-kindness, otherwise sadness will harden the heart and lead it more deeply into despair.

Bernard of Clairvaux[14]

The attitude in which the benefits of God are recalled with gladness and thanksgiving involves a twofold grace: it lightens the burdens of the present life, makes them more supportable for those who can give themselves with joy to the work of praising God; and nothing more appropriately represents on earth the state of life in the heavenly fatherland than spontaneity in this outpouring of praise.

We read in the Book of Wisdom: 'Think of the Lord with goodness, seek him in simplicity of heart'. You will all the more easily achieve this if you let your mind dwell frequently, even continually, on the memory of God's bountifulness. Otherwise, how will you fulfill Saint Paul's advice, 'In all things give thanks to God', if your heart will have lost sight of those things for which thanks are due?

Bernard of Clairvaux[15]

Happy the person who at each gift of grace returns to him in whom is the fullness of all graces. If we show ourselves grateful for graces received, we make room for grace in ourselves, that we may deserve to receive even greater graces than in the past. For the only thing that hinders us from advancing in the spiritual life is our ingratitude.

Let us humble ourselves more and more under the all-powerful hand of God most high and let us especially strive to keep far from this most wicked vice of ingratitude, so that, living with full devotion in thanksgiving, we may gain the grace of our God, which alone can save our souls. Let us show that we are not ungrateful, not only in word or in speech, but in deed and in truth, for it is not saying thanks, but giving thanks which the Lord our God requires of us.

Bernard of Clairvaux[16]

Bless me, most loving Jesus,
bless me and have mercy on me in the
loving-kindness of your most gracious heart.
May my soul choose to know nothing apart from you,
that, disciplined by your grace and
instructed by the anointing of your Spirit,
I may progress well, passionately, and powerfully
in the school of your love.

Gertrud of Helfta[17]

All the exercises, all the aspects of love which we have considered, coalesce and reinforce each other:

'Happy is the one who shall abide in wisdom'. To achieve this wisdom of continuing in wisdom, it is most important, I think, not readily to allow restlessness or any kind of slight provocation to keep you away from any of the exercises of wisdom: the divine office, private prayer, lectio, the appointed daily labor or the practice of silence.

For the praises of wisdom are sung at the completion of the office. 'My lips will rejoice', says the Holy Man, 'when they shall have sung to you'.

As for private prayer, you know from daily experience that it too is better at the end than it is at the beginning. This is so that you may have confidence in the advice of the Lord, given so often and recommended by so much example, to be persevering in prayer.

Again when you sit down to read and you do not really read, or if before you even begin to read you put the book down again, what good do you think that will do you? If you do not continue with the Scriptures so as to become familiar with them through assiduous study, when do you think they will open themselves to you? To one who has love of the word, we are told, understanding shall be given and he will abound; but from one who has not, what knowledge he may have by way of natural endowment, will be taken away because of his negligence.

Then with regard to manual work, surely you have learned enough about this, have you not, to know that, like the wage given to the workers, consolation is often reserved to the end of the work? And of course when we come to silence a promise is given by the Prophet when he says: 'In silence and in hope shall your strength be'.

For if you cultivate holiness in silence and following the advice of Jeremiah, you wait in silence for the salvation of the Lord, then secretly in the midst of the silence the all-powerful Word of God will leap down to you from his royal throne. The waters of Siloe which flow silently will inundate the valley of your quiet and peaceful heart like a gently flowing stream. And this you will experience not once but many times, if only your silence is the cultivation of holiness, that is, if you meditate on holiness so that you may continue in the Scriptures as I have suggested, and in your mind consider the all-seeing eye of God.

Guerric of Igny[18]

*At the summit of the discipline, the disappoint-
ments, and the gratitude is love, the greatest
virtue which somehow contains all the other
virtues.*

It is by love that we especially approach God, indeed, by which we cleave to God and are conformed to him. In it the fullness of all perfection resides.

Aelred of Rievaulx[19]

Other virtues are like a carriage for someone weary, food for the traveller's journey, a lamp for those groping in darkness, and weapons for those waging battle. But charity, which permits other virtues to be virtues, must exist in all the virtues. It is full light at journey's end, and the perfect crown for the victor. For what is faith, but a carriage to carry us to our fatherland? What is hope, but food for the journey to support us in the miseries of this life? What are the four virtues—temperance, prudence, fortitude, and justice—but the weapons with which we wage battle? But when death will be fully swallowed up in charity, which will reach its perfection only in the vision of God, there will be no faith for those who begin in faith, because there is no need to believe in One who is seen and loved. Nor will hope exist because for someone who embraces God with the arms of charity there remains nothing to hope for.

Aelred of Rievaulx[20]

By love and charity, the Cistercians mean a persevering love. A transitory affection is of no avail. Love is not love unless it perseveres.

It is perseverance which is the glory, the perfection, and, as it were, the virtue of all the virtues. Now charity is also a virtue which is much praised—a virtue, indeed, which deserves much praise for it is the life and virtue of the other virtues—but the virtue of charity is patience, and the virtue of patience is perseverance. Charity without patience is not true charity but an imitation, and imitation charity flourishes in good times but collapses in adversity. Patience without perseverance is inconstant and feeble; it is born in adversity, but it weakens in the course of time, and with prolonged effort it succumbs. But perseverance neither flourishes, nor falls, nor weakens, nor succumbs. It is as if all the other virtues were running in a race, but that which takes the prize is the straight course of perseverance.

Baldwin of Forde[21]

The will to persevere will be strengthened, rather than shaken, by difficulties. An effortless and untried love lacks staying power.

It is good for me to be troubled, Lord, as long as you are with me, better than reigning without you, of feasting

without you, of being glorified without you. It is good
for me to embrace you in tribulation, to have you with
me in the furnace, better than being without you even
in heaven. 'For whom have I in heaven but you? And
there is nothing on earth that I desire beside you'. 'The
furnace tests gold, and the trial of tribulation just men'.
There, yes, there you are present with them, Lord. You
are there in the midst of those gathered in your name,
as you once deigned to appear in the fiery furnace with
the three young men even to a heathen, so that he might
say 'the appearance of the fourth is like the son of God'.
Why should we tremble, why should we hesitate, why
flee this furnace? The fire rages, but the Lord is with us
in tribulation. 'If God is with us who can be against us?'
If he snatches us out of their hands, who can grab us out
of his? Is there anyone who can pluck us out of his hand?

Bernard of Clairvaux[22]

I will love you, good Jesus.
I will love you, my strength,
whom I cannot love without your
help and cannot love as you deserve.
May my endeavors be directed to you without reserve
and may they not be diverted and
distracted by any other affection.
May I be wholly carried to you by my desires, good God.
Draw me to yourself
that I may require no stimulus of fear
and that perfect charity may
banish any recourse to fear.

Gilbert of Hoyland[23]

Sources and Scriptural References

1. *On the Song of Songs* 25.7; CF 7:55.
   Gn 1:26; 2 Cor 4:16; Ps 45:14; 2 Cor 1:12.
2. *The Mirror of Charity* 2.18.53; CF 17:200.
3. Spiritual Exercise 5; CF 49:84.
4. *On the Song of Songs* 13.1; CF 4:87.
5. *On the Song of Songs* 22.10–11; CF 7:23–24.
   1 Cor 1:30; Ws 8:7; Is 32:17.
6. Sermon for the Birthday of Mary 22.21.
   Ws 8:7.
7. Tractate 3: CF 38:92.
   Jn 14:23–24.
8. Tractate 9/2; CF 41:41–42.
   Mt 11:29–30.
9. Sermon 59.11; CF 44:181.
10. Sermon 30.14; CF 66.
    Heb 10:36; Jas 1:4.
11. Sermon 4.3–7 (abridged); CF 8:26–29.
    Mk 1:3; Is 40:4; Ws 1:4; Ps 119:105; Ps 40:8; Prov 24:16; Ps
    146:8; Ps 17:5; Ps 138:24; Jn 14:6.
12. Sermon 91.7; CF 46:104.
    Eph 4:5; Mt 5:24.
13. *On the Song of Songs* 21.10; CF 7:11.
    Ps 34:12; Ps 86:11; Ps 2:11.
14. *On the Song of Songs* 11.2; CF 4:70.
    Ps 37:4.
15. *On the Song of Songs* 11.1–2; CF 4:69–71.
    Zep 2:17; Ws 1:1; 1 Th 5:18.
16. *Occasional Sermons* 27.8; CF 68.
    1 Pt 5:6; Jm 1:21; 1 Jn 3:18.
17. Spiritual Exercise 2; CF 49:37.
18. Sermon 22.5; CF 32:5–7.
    Si 14:22; Ps 71:23; Lk 18:1; Mt 23:12; Mt 20:10; Is 30:15; Lam
    3:26; Ws 18:15; Is 8:6; Is 32:17; Si 14:22.
19. *The Mirror of Charity* 3.36.96; CF 17:288.
20. *The Mirror of Charity* 1.31.88; CF 17:140–141.
    Ws 8:7; 1 Cor 15:54.

21. Tractate 4; CF 38:105.
    Mt 10:22; 1 Cor 8:24.
22. *Sermons on Psalm 90* 17.4; CF 25:257–258.
    Ps 72:24; Si 27:6; Mt 18:20; Dn 3:92; Rom 8:31; Jn 10:28.
23. Sermon 19.6; CF 20:245.

7 ❧

Growing in Love

As in any school, so in the school of love, the students do not reach their goal in a single step. There are stages of growth we must follow. The Cistercians have a number of ways of describing the stages of this growth in love and conformity to Christ.

THERE ARE THREE STAGES of the soul's growth in love, of its advance toward perfection. First comes the forgiveness of sins, then the grace that follows on good deeds, and finally that contemplative gift by which a kind and beneficent Lord shows himself to the soul with as much clarity as bodily frailty can endure.

These three stages may be described metaphorically—and scripturally—as a kiss, 'a sign and incentive to an inward union'[1]: moved by love, we kiss the Lord's feet, we kiss his hand, and finally we kiss his mouth:

The heartfelt desire to admit one's guilt brings a person down in lowliness before God, as it were to his feet; the heartfelt devotion of a worshiper finds in God renewal and refreshment, the touch, as it were, of his hand; and the delights of contemplation lead on to that ecstatic repose that is the fruit of the kiss of his mouth.

Bernard of Clairvaux[2]

As we grow in love, our attachment to God changes from the relationship of slaves to their master to one of hirelings to their employer, and finally to that of sons to their father.

A person can acknowledge that the Lord is powerful, that the Lord is good to him, and that the Lord is simply good. The first is the love of a slave who fears for himself; the second is that of a hireling who thinks only of himself; the third is that of a son who honors his father. The one, therefore, who fears and the one who covets do so for themselves. Love is found only in the son. It does not seek its own advantage. For this reason I think this virtue is meant in the text: 'The law of the Lord is spotless, it converts the soul', for it alone can turn the mind away from loving one's self and the world, and fix it on loving God. Neither fear nor love of self can change the soul. At times they change one's appearance or deeds; they can never alter one's character. Sometimes even a slave can do God's work, but it is not done freely; he is still base. The hireling can do it also, but not freely; he is seen to be lured by his own cupidity. Let the slave have his own law, the very fear which binds him; let the hireling's be the desire for gain which restrains him when he is attracted and enticed by temptation. But neither of these is without fault nor can either convert souls. Love converts souls because it makes them act willingly.

Bernard of Clairvaux[3]

The relationship can also be described in terms of our human faculties.

The love of God in the christian soul has three stages. The first is sensual or animal; the second, rational; the third is spiritual or intellectual. The Lord speaks of them in this way in the gospel: 'You shall love the Lord your God with your whole heart, with your whole soul and with all your strength'. The first is signified by the word *heart*, that is, by a small organ of weak flesh, and it expresses itself in a loyal feeling of love for the humanity of the Savior; the second by the word *soul*, by which that first love is given soul and life; for at this stage a person begins to seek out the mysteries of faith and the power of the sacraments with humble devotion; and the third by the words *all your strength*; for at this stage, however far you have advanced, you will still be able to say: 'And I said, Now have I begun'.

The first takes such pleasure in the contemplation and enjoyment of the humanity of Christ that Christ may with some reason say to those who are at it, 'It is good for you that I go away'. By now, at this second stage, a person's heart is aflame, though, being still on the journey, her eyes are as yet prevented from seeing Christ as he speaks to her and explains the Scriptures to her. At the third stage, a person says, having gained full confidence, 'And if once we knew Christ in a human way, that is no longer how we know him', which the first person cannot say at all and the second hardly.

But let us examine more closely the riches in which all three abound. The first resists temptations; the second resists heresies, while the third sings 'I will lie down in him and rest in peace'. In the first is forgiveness of sins and the cleansing of vices; in the second, the practice of virtues; in the third the perfection of virtues and a clinging to and enjoyment of the highest good.

The first hears the word of those who daily say to her 'Where is your God?'; the second remembers those things and pours out her soul. The third goes to the place of the wonderful tent, ascending to the house of God. The first is in service to faith, the second to hope, the third to charity; and as faith gives us birth in God, hope feeds us and charity completes our maturity, so the first step of love in us consecrates human feeling to God; the second throws off the old man in his actions and puts on the new man, created by God in the justice and holiness of truth; the third brings us to maturity, brings us into conformity with God in both purity of mind and holiness of life.

William of Saint Thierry[4]

Our love must begin with the flesh, and when this is set in order, our love advances by fixed degrees, led on by grace, until it is consummated in the spirit, for 'Not what is spiritual comes first, but what is animal, then what is spiritual'. It is necessary that we bear first the likeness of an earthly being, then that of a heavenly being. Thus we first love our self for our own sake because we are carnal and sensitive to nothing but our self. Then when we see we cannot subsist by ourself, we begin to seek for God by faith and to love him as necessary to ourself. So in the second degree of love, we love God for our sake and not for God's sake. When, forced by our own needs, we begin to honor God and care for him by thinking of him, reading about him, praying to him, and obeying him, God reveals himself gradually in this kind of familiarity and consequently becomes lovable. When we taste how sweet God is, we pass to the third degree of love in which we love God not now because of our self but because of God. No doubt we remain a long time in this degree, and I doubt if we ever attain the fourth degree during this life, that is, if we ever love only for God's sake.

Bernard of Clairvaux[5]

May the faithful God,
the true Amen, who does not grow faint,
make me thirst fervently for the dear Amen
with which he himself affects the soul;
taste with pleasure the sweet Amen
with which he himself refreshes the soul;
be consummated in happiness by that saving Amen
with which he himself perfects the soul.

Gertrud of Helfta[6]

For the Cistercians, the touchstone of our pro-gress towards God in the school of love is not mystical experience, but moral improvement:

If I feel that my eyes are opened to understand the Scrip-tures, so that I am enlightened from above to preach the word of wisdom from the heart or reveal the mysteries

of God, or if riches from on high are showered upon me
so that in my soul fruits of meditation are produced, I
have no doubt that the Bridegroom is with me. For these
are gifts of the Word, and it is of his fullness that we have
received these gifts. Again if I am filled with a feeling of
humility rich with devotion whereby love of the truth
I have received produces in me so urgent a hatred and
contempt for vanity that I cannot be inflamed with pride
by reason of knowledge, nor elated by the frequency of
heavenly visitations, then truly I am aware of fatherly
activity and do not doubt the Father's presence. But if I
continue as far as I can to respond to this condescension
in worthy disposition and action, and the grace of God in
me has not been fruitless, then the Father will make his
abode with me to nourish me, as the Son will teach me.

Bernard of Clairvaux[7]

You ask then how I knew God was present, when his
ways can in no way be traced? He is life and power, and
as soon as he enters in, he awakens my slumbering soul;
he stirs and soothes and pierces my heart, for before
it was hard as stone, and diseased. So he has begun to
pluck out and destroy, to build up and to plant, to water
dry places and illuminate dark ones; to open what was
closed and to warm what was cold; to make the crooked
straight and the rough places smooth, so that my soul
may bless the Lord, and all that is within me may praise
his holy name.

When he came to me, he never made known his coming
by any signs, not by sight, not by sound, not by touch.
It was not by any movement of his that I recognized his
coming; it was not by any of my senses that I perceived

he had penetrated to the depths of my being. Only by the movement of my heart did I perceive his presence; and I knew the power of his might because my faults were put to flight and my human yearnings brought into subjection. I have marvelled at the depth of his wisdom when my secret faults have been revealed and made visible; at the very slightest amendment of my way of life I have experienced his goodness and mercy; in the renewal and remaking of the spirit of my mind, that is of my inmost being, I have perceived the excellence of his glorious beauty, and when I contemplate all these things I am filled with awe and wonder at his manifold greatness.

Bernard of Clairvaux[8]

As our love grows and likeness is restored, we acquire a taste for the good. This savor shares in the great quality called wisdom. It was a link the Cistercians saw in the similarity of the latin words sapor *(taste) and* sapientia *(wisdom).*

If anyone defines wisdom as the love of virtue, I think you are not far from the truth. For where there is love, there is no toil, but a taste. Perhaps *sapientia*, that is wisdom, is derived from *sapor*, that is taste, because, when it is added to virtue, like some seasoning, it adds taste to something which by itself is tasteless and bitter. I think it would be permissible to define wisdom as a taste for goodness. We lost this taste almost from the creation of our human race. When the old serpent's poison infected the palate of our heart, because the fleshly sense prevailed, the soul began to lose her taste for goodness, and a depraved taste crept in. 'A person's imagination and thoughts are evil from his youth', that is, as a result of the folly of the first woman. So it was folly which drove the taste for good from the woman, because the serpent's malice outwitted the woman's folly. But the reason which caused the malice to appear for a time victorious, is the same reason why it suffers eternal defeat. For see! It is again the heart and body of a woman which wisdom fills and makes fruitful so that, as by a woman we were deformed into folly, so by a woman we may be reformed to wisdom. Now wisdom always prevails over malice in the minds which it has entered, and drives out the taste for evil which the other has brought to it, by introducing something better. When wisdom enters, it makes the carnal sense taste flat, it purifies the understanding, cleanses and heals the palate of the heart. Thus, when the palate is clean, it tastes the good, it tastes wisdom itself, and there is nothing better.

How many good actions are performed without the doers having any taste for them, because they are compelled to do them by their way of life or by some circumstance or necessity? And on the contrary many who do evil with no taste for it are led by fear or desire for something, rather than because they relish evil. But those who act in accordance with the affection of their hearts are either wise, and delight in goodness because they have a taste for it, or else they are wicked, and take pleasure in wrong-doing, even if they are not moved by any hope of gain. For what is malice but a taste for evil? Happy is the mind which is protected by a taste for good and a hatred of evil, for this is what it means to be reformed to wisdom, and to know by experience and to rejoice in the victory of wisdom. For in nothing is the victory of wisdom over malice more evident than when the taste for evil—which is what malice is—is purged away, and the mind's inmost taste senses that it is deeply filled with sweetness. It looks to virtue to sustain tribulations with fortitude, and to wisdom to rejoice in those tribulations. To strengthen your heart and to wait upon the Lord—that is virtue; to taste and see that the Lord is good—that is wisdom.

Bernard of Clairvaux[9]

By its anointing, wisdom teaches all things. Then, by having affixed the seal of God's goodness to us, it imprints and conforms to itself by this anointing everything calmed and gentled within us. If it finds any hardness, any rigidity, it pounds and crushes it until this person, having received this wholesome happiness of God and having been strengthened by the spirit of wisdom, joyfully sings to God: 'The light of your countenance, O Lord, has shone upon us. You have given gladness to my heart'. For this also is why the Lord says: 'This is eternal life, that they may know you, the only true God, and Jesus Christ whom you have sent'. O blessed knowledge, wherein is contained eternal life!

William of Saint Thierry[10]

Wisdom, the culmination of our growth in the virtues, reflects our obedience and conformity to the divine Image and leads from the turmoil of disobedience and disorder to inner peace.

After advancing for a long time in the gradual stages of virtue and exercising herself strenuously in the labor of spiritual discipline, then indeed the soul finds she has received a hundred-fold in peace and tranquillity of heart,

in serenity and security, in the delight of righteousness
and the ineffable sweetness of spiritual joy.

Baldwin of Forde[11]

My Lord Jesus Christ,
may your peace be with me.
In you, O Jesus, true peace,
may I have peace upon peace eternally.
Through you may I come to that peace
which surpasses all understanding—
there where, in gladness, I may see you in yourself.

Gertrud of Helfta[12]

Sources and Scriptural References

1. *Exposition on the Song of Songs* 30; CF 6: 25
2. *On the Song of Songs* 4.1.4; CF 4:22–23.
   Sg 1:1.
3. *On Loving God* 12.35; CF 13:126.
   Ps 118:1; 1 Cor 13:5; Ps 19:8.
4. *A Brief Commentary on the Song of Songs* 1–6 (abridged);
   CS 156:277–80.
   Mt 22:7; Ps 77:11; Jn 16:17; Lk 24:15–32; 1 Cor 5:16; Ps 4:9;
   Ps 42:4–5; Eph 4:22–24.
5. *On Loving God* 39; CF 13:130–131.
   1 Cor 15:46, 49; Heb 11:6; Ps 34:9.
6. Spiritual Exercise 1; CF 49:32.
7. *On the Song of Songs* 69.6; CF 40:32–33.
8. *On the Song of Songs* 74.6; CF 40:91–92.
   Rom 11:33; Heb 4:12; Sg 4:9; Ez 11:19; Jer 1:10; Ps 103:1;
   Eph 1:13; Qo 7:25; Ps 19:13; Eph 4:23; Ps 50:2; Ps 150:2.
9. *On the Song of Songs* 85.8–9; CF 40:204–205.
   Gn 18:21; Ws 7:30; Ps 27:14; Ps 34:9.

10. *The Nature and Dignity of Love* 31; CF 30:91–92.
    1 Jn 2:27; Ps 51:14; Ps 4:6–7; Jn 17:3.
11. Tractate 14; CF 41:153.
    Mk 10:30.
12. Spiritual Exercise 1; CF 49:29.

8 ～

Loving Others

As the author of the First Letter of John reminds us, anyone who claims to love God while scorning or remaining indifferent to the persons with whom he lives, suffers from a blindness that will hold him back from responding to and accepting the love of God.

*T*HE SOUL RETURNS and is converted to the Word to be reformed by him and conformed to him. In what way? In love—for Paul says, 'Be imitators of God, like dear children, and walk in love, as Christ also has loved you'.

Bernard of Clairvaux[1]

Just as love unceasingly embraces God, the creator of all, with outstretched arms, so it should incline to the needs of creatures, loving good and bad alike, and should extend itself with a generous merciful heart.

Beatrice of Nazareth[2]

*Our love has three objects: our self, God, and
other persons—for we are told to love our neighbor as our self. But love is one, and these three
expressions of love are closely united:*

Although there is an evident distinction between love
of God, love of neighbor, and love of self, a marvelous
bond nevertheless does exist among the three, so that
each is found in all, and all in each. None of them can
be possessed without all, and when one wavers they
all diminish. Someone who does not love his neighbor
or God does not love himself, and someone who does
not love his neighbor as himself does not love himself.
Furthermore, someone who does not love his neighbor is
proven not to love God. For 'how can a person who does
not love the brother he sees love God whom he does not
see?' These three loves are engendered by one another,
nourished by one another, and fanned into flame by one
another. Then they are all brought to perfection together.

Aelred of Rievaulx[3]

*A modern Cistercian has commented that 'love
grows by loving, and loves by growing'[4] Love has
a dynamism of its own. If it is growing, love will
affect all our relationships. It will enable us to*

live in an orderly, friendly, and humble manner: orderly toward yourself, friendly toward your neighbor,
and humbly toward God. In an orderly way, so that in
your whole way of life you are careful to pay heed to your
ways, both in God's sight and your neighbor's, guard-
ing yourself from sin, and your neighbor from scandal.
With friendliness, so that you strive to be loved and to

love, to show yourself gentle and friendly, to support the weaknesses of others not only patiently, but gladly. With humility, so that when you have done all these things, you may strive to blow away the spirit of vanity, which tends to arise from them, and whenever you perceive it, to totally refuse consent.

Bernard of Clairvaux[5]

Our love for God and our love for our neighbor converge in Christ, who is both divine and human.

Let this be the model to which your lives conform: to be in thought and desire at home in the everlasting fatherland with Christ, and yet shirk no kind service that can be done for Christ's sake during the toilsome journey through life; to be willing to follow Christ the Lord on his upward journey to the Father and thus become clearsighted, purified and revived in mediation, not to refuse to follow Christ's going down to one's brothers and sisters, and through such activity being everywhere by turns to everyone. Nothing that may be done for Christ's sake must be despised, and nothing must be desired that is not for Christ's sake; Christ is ever the one and only source of that longing for him that finds expression both in the leisure that concerns itself with Christ as one, and in the willing service of many where Christ is manifold.

Isaac of Stella[6]

The more we love others, the greater becomes our capacity for loving God.

The soul must grow and expand, that she may be roomy enough for God. Her width is her love, if we accept what the Apostle says: 'Widen your hearts in love'. The soul, being a spirit, does not admit of material expansion, but grace confers gifts on her that nature is not equipped to bestow. Her growth and expansion must be understood in a spiritual sense; it is her virtue that increases, not her substance. Even her glory is increased. And finally she grows and advances toward 'mature manhood, to the measure of the stature of the fullness of Christ'. Eventually she becomes 'a holy temple in the Lord'.

The capacity of anyone's soul is judged by the amount of love he possesses; hence one who loves much is great, one who loves a little is small, one who has no love is nothing, as Paul said: 'If I have not love, I am nothing'. But if one begins to acquire some love however, if one tries at least to love those who love him, and salutes the brethren and others who salute him, I may no longer describe such a one as nothing because some love must be present in the give and take of social life. In the words of the Lord, however, what more is he doing than others? When I discover a love as mediocre as this, I cannot call such a person noble or great; he is obviously narrowminded and mean.

But if his love expands and continues to advance till it outgrows these narrow, servile confines, and finds itself in the open ranges where love is freely given in full liberty of spirit; when from the generous bounty of his goodwill he strives to reach out to all his neighbors, loving each of them as himself, surely one may no longer query, 'What more are you doing than others?' Indeed he has made himself vast. His heart is filled with a love that embraces everybody, even those to whom it is not tied by the inseparable bonds of family relationship; a love that is not allured by any hope of personal gain, that possesses nothing it is obliged to restore, that bears no burden of debt whatever, apart from that one of which it is said: 'Owe no one anything, except to love one another'.

Progressing further still, you may endeavor to take the kingdom of love by force, until by this holy warfare you succeed in possessing it even to its farthest bounds. Instead of shutting off your affections from your enemies, you will do good to those who hate you, you will pray for those who persecute and slander you, you will strive to be peaceful even with those who hate peace. Then the width, height and beauty of your soul will be the width, height and beauty of heaven itself, and in this heaven, he who is supreme and immense and glorious will be pleased to dwell.

Bernard of Clairvaux[7]

The person whose soul has been enlarged
through love may be described as

someone who takes pity and lends, who is disposed to be compassionate, quick to render assistance, who believes that there is more happiness in giving than in receiving, who easily forgives but is not easily angered, who will never seek to be avenged, and will in all things take thought for his neighbor's needs as if they were his own. Such a person is overflowing with affectionate kindness, making himself all things to all men yet pricing his deeds like something discarded in order to be ever and everywhere ready to supply to others what they need, in a word, so dead to himself that he lives only for others.

Bernard of Clairvaux[8]

Those who love one another

are pleasant and temperate, without grudging; they neither deceive nor attack nor offend another; they never
exalt themselves nor promote themselves at another's
expense, but offer their services as generously as they
accept those of others.

Bernard of Clairvaux[9]

Their affection towards everyone is reverent, their con-
sensus in good is agreeable. Their encounter is in cheer-
fulness, their dwelling together in grace, their going out
of their way in a manifestation of charity. They do not
look out for their own concerns but for those of everyone
else. And if it is possible, even in those things which
are difficult, they often make everyone else's concerns
their own. To this end they easily adapt everything to
whatever the highest law has ordained since they have
received the pledge or the seal of the Holy Spirit.

William of Saint Thierry[10]

*Those who love one another in this way 'dwell
together in unity'. The Cistercians extolled the
blessedness of living in community.*

'The multitude of believers had but one heart and one
soul; no one said that any of the things he possessed was
his own, but they had everything in common'. What
makes community life, therefore, is one heart, one soul,
and having everything in common. Such a life is an
earthly copy—so far as human weakness allows—of the
life of the angels.

Since they have but one heart and one soul and all things in common, there is concord and unanimity throughout, and they always put the general profit and the common good before their own individual convenience. They so far renounce themselves and what is theirs that none of them, if indeed he is truly one of them, whether in making decisions or in giving advice, presumes to make a stubborn defence of his own opinion, nor to strive hard after his own will and the desires of his own heart, nor to have the least thing which could be called his own. They live not by their own spirit, but by the Spirit of God. It is he who leads them to be sons of God, and it is he who is their love, their bond, and their communion. The greater their love, the stronger is their bond and the more perfect is their communion: and conversely, the greater their communion, the stronger is their bond and the more perfect is their love.

Baldwin of Forde[11]

There is nothing in human life better than mutual love nor anything sweeter than holy fellowship. To love and be loved is a sweet exchange, the joy of one's whole life, the recompense of blessedness. What can be lacking in the sweetness of this good and pleasant dwelling, this place where God dwells and where he rests? 'God is in his holy place, God, who makes those of one mind to dwell in a house'.

Baldwin of Forde[12]

Is it not a foretaste of blessedness thus to love and thus to be loved? Thus to help and thus to be helped? In this way from the sweetness of fraternal charity we wing our flight aloft to that more sublime splendor of divine love, and by the ladder of love we mount to the embrace of Christ himself; and again we descend to the love of neighbor, there pleasantly to rest.

Aelred of Rievaulx[13]

Sources and Scriptural References

1. *On the Song of Songs* 83.2; CF 40:182.
   Sg 7:10; Eph 5:1.
2. *Life of Beatrice* 15; CF 50:333.
3. *The Mirror of Charity* 3.2.3,5; CF 17:223-224.
   1 Jn 4:20.
4. Eugene Boylan ocso, *Difficulties in Mental Prayer* (Westminster, MD: Newman, 1948) p. 47.
5. First Sermon for Saints Peter and Paul 4; CF 52:102.
6. Sermon 11.6; CF 11:101.
   1 Cor 9:22.
7. *On the Song of Songs* 27.10-11; CF 7:83-84.
   2 Cor 6:13; Eph 4:13; Eph 2:21; 1 Cor 13:2; Lk 6:32; Mt 5:47; Phil 4:15; Mt 5:47; Mt 19:19; Rom 13:8; Mt 11:12; 1 Jn 3:17; Mt 5:44; Ps 120:7.
8. *On the Song of Songs* 12.1; CF 4:78.
   Ps 112:5; Acts 20:35; 1 Cor 9:22.
9. *On the Song of Songs* 23.6; CF 7:30-31.
   2 Cor 7:2; Phil 4:15.
10. *The Nature and Dignity of Love* 23; CF 30:81-82.
    2 Cor 1:22.
11. Tractate 15; CF 41:171.
    Acts 4:32; Rom 8:14.
12. Tractate 5; CF 38:141-142.
    Ps 133:1; Ps 68:5-6.
13. *On Spiritual Friendship* 3.127; CF 5:129.

9 ✬

Love of God

When they speak of the love of God—the love that comes from God and is given to God—the Cistercians become especially eloquent. God's love is a reality so vast that it can never be wholly apprehended. Yet it can be endlessly delighted in.

O WORD summing up and abbreviating with equity!

O word of charity, word of love,
word of endearment, word of total inner perfection!
O summarizing word which can lack nothing,
abbreviating word on which 'depend
the whole law and the prophets'.

Aelred of Rievaulx[1]

Just as it is impossible for fire not to burn, so it is impossible for charity not to love. Love, after all, is a fire, and to love, therefore, is to burn. Fire does not contain itself within itself, but always seems to be trying to reach out for whatever it is burning. It has no wish to live only

in itself, and it therefore shares its heat with the things
it has touched and burned. In just the same way, love,
by a certain instinctive movement, longs to pour itself
forth and transfer the good it possesses to someone it
loves with all its love; it longs to have it in common, to
take the other as a companion and to share its possession
with him.

Baldwin of Forde[2]

What could be more violent than love? Love prevails even
with God. What could be so non-violent? It is love. What
force is there, I ask, which advances so violently toward
victory, yet is so unresisting to violence? For Christ emp-
tied himself, so that you might know that it was the
fullness of love which was outpoured, that his loftiness
was laid low and that his unique nature made to be your
fellow.

Bernard of Clairvaux[3]

Love boils over, does not contain itself, overflows itself,
rivals immensity, while it knows not how to set a limit to
its affections. It is oil which cannot stop its flow until no
other container is available, except that not even then can
it be checked. Love shows a characteristic of new wine
which, by fermenting as it is born and by wantonness as
it ages, bubbles up and overflows unable to contain itself,
always seething and fermenting with fresh affection.
In its infirmity, love does not excuse but accuses itself.
Nothing is enough for love, nothing less than itself. Love
cannot be satisfied with itself and yet love can feed only
on itself; it is food delicious enough for itself. Love wants
nothing more than to love. What will a person give in
exchange for love? What will one give or what will one

receive? Nothing is imparted more graciously than love, nothing is experienced more gently. Love is delicious in desire and in enjoyment; love is delicious in joy and sorrow. Truly love is sweet and only love is sweet and all love is sweet but no love exists to compare with the love of Christ, for his beauty is above all beauty.

Gilbert of Hoyland[4]

This love engages our whole being, and every aspect and dimension of it.

'You shall love the Lord your God with your whole heart, your whole soul and your whole strength'. It seems to me that the love of the heart relates to a certain warmth of affection, the love of the soul to energy or judgment of reason, and the love of strength can refer to constancy and vigor of spirit. So love the Lord your God with the full and deep affection of your heart, love him with your mind wholly awake and discreet, love him with all your strength, so much so that you would not even fear to die for love of him. As it is written: 'For love is strong as death, jealousy is bitter as hell'.

Let your love be strong and constant, neither yielding to fear nor cowering at hard work. Let us love affectionately, discreetly, intensely. We know that the love of the heart, which we have said is affectionate, is sweet indeed, but liable to be led astray if it lacks the love of the soul. And the love of the soul is wise indeed, but fragile without that love which is called the love of strength.

Bernard of Clairvaux[5]

Just as we should love God with all our heart, all our soul and all our mind, so we should love all of him. He is wholly lovable, wholly desirable, and in him can be found nothing worthy of hatred, nothing unworthy of love.

O God of goodness and liberality;
O God, so lovable and desirable, so worthy of our love;
O God who is love;
O God who is charity;
O God of so sweet a nature!

Baldwin of Forde[6]

It is love for the sake of which everything should be done or not done, changed or not changed; it is the beginning for the sake of which and the end to which everything should be directed. Nothing that is really done for its sake and conforms to it need ever deserve blame. May he generously bestow it upon us, for apart from him we cannot please him, and separated from him we have no power to do anything at all.

Isaac of Stella[7]

The height of our love for God is when it hopes for the heights and desires the sublimities of glory, not in this world, but in God, in him who says, 'When I am lifted up from the earth, I will draw all things to myself', and to whom the bridegroom says, 'Draw me after you'.

Its depth is when we strive for the truth for the sake of God and choose to be abased, following the example of him who said, 'I have chosen to be abased'. We are shown by this that whoever abases himself has no wish to choose honor.

Love is long when it perseveres to the end or, rather, when it has no end, for love never ceases. It is wide when it is mindful of God's benevolence and kindness, when it continually delights in him, both in adversity and prosperity, when it rejoices in him and cries to him always in joy and exultation, in all places and with all gladness, when it is not restrained by faint-heartedness or grumbling. The breadth of love is the expansion of the heart, which is also its delight in righteousness.

Baldwin of Forde[8]

Someone who loves you, Lord, makes no mistake in his choice, for nothing is better than you. His hope is not cheated, since nothing is loved with greater reward.

He need not fear exceeding the limit,
since in loving you no limit is set.
He does not dread death, the disrupter of
worldly friendships, since life never dies.
In loving you, he fears no offense, for none
exists but the abandonment of love itself.
No suspicion gets in the way, since you
judge by the testimony of conscience itself.
Here is joy, because fear is banished.
Here is tranquillity, because anger is curbed.
Here is security, because the world is scorned.

Aelred of Rievaulx[9]

*To know God is to love God; and to love God is
to know him ever better and better. Knowledge*

of God and love of God grow together and func-
tion together, becoming ever more closely inter-
twined so that, as the Cistercians like to put it,
'love itself is knowledge', a knowledge born of
experience.

The sight for seeing God, the natural light of the soul
created by the Author of nature, is charity. There are,
however, two eyes in this sight: love and reason. . . .
Reason can only see God in what he is not, while love
can rest only in what he is. . . . Reason is able to discover
what God is only to the extent that it discovers what he
is not . . . Love, putting aside what God is not, rejoices to
love itself in what he is. From him, love has come forth,
and it naturally yearns for its own beginning. Reason
has the greater sobriety. Love the greater happiness. . . .
When they help each other—when reason instructs love
and love enlightens reason, when reason effaces itself
before the energy of love and love accepts the restraints
of reason—then they can accomplish great things.

William of Saint Thierry[10]

You, O God, are the supreme Wisdom, and to know you is
perfect understanding. It is through love that we know
you, for love itself is knowledge, and if someone does
not love you then he does not yet know who you are
in the way that he should. However much he prides
himself on the glory of his brilliant eloquence, however
much he extols himself for his knowledge of marvels
and wonders, however much he displays his abundance
of desirable things, if he does not love you, then he is
foolish and stupid. If he does not love you, he is a beggar
and a pauper, for the riches of salvation are wisdom and

knowledge. But the wisdom with which someone who loves you savors you is more precious than all riches, and of all the things that we desire, there is none that can compare with it.

Baldwin of Forde[11]

Eternal life is knowing the true God;
the true way to it is to love with one's whole heart.
Love, then, is the way, truth the life;
truth is the image,
love the likeness;
love is the price, truth is the prize;
by love we make our journey,
in truth we stand fast.
Moreover, since love will never come to an end,
when truth is attained love is not at an end,
but the life with the truth that comes of love
and the love that comes of truth will be
supremely satisfying and will never stop.

Isaac of Stella[12]

Everyone possesses you just insofar as he loves you.

William of Saint Thierry[13]

*Love gathers into itself all other human affec-
tions and all virtues.*

Love is a great reality, and if it returns to its beginning and goes back to its origin, seeking its source again, it will always draw afresh from it, and thereby flow freely.

Love is the only one of the motions of the soul, of its senses and affections, in which the creature can respond to its Creator, even if not as an equal, and repay his favor in some similar way. For example, if God is angry with me, am I to be angry in return? No, indeed, but I shall tremble with fear and ask pardon. So also, if he accuses me, I shall not accuse him in return, but rather justify him. Nor, if he judges me, shall I judge him, but I shall adore him; and in saving me he does not ask to be saved by me; nor does he who sets all men free need to be set free by me. If he commands, I must obey, and not demand his service or obedience. Now you see how different love is, for when God loves, he desires nothing but to be loved, since he loves us for no other reason than to be loved, for he knows that those who love him are blessed in their very love.

Bernard of Clairvaux[14]

O love, you stand at the right hand of the king, filling all things with your sweetness. You rule everything with your laws, you teach everything with your doctrine, you beautify everything with your glory. How sweet, how strong, how radiant, how glorious you are in that kingdom of your glory! In that kingdom of yours, you have imposed silence on all tongues, so that you alone may speak. You have annulled all laws and command-ments, so that you alone are the eternal law, the new commandment, the new covenant. You have folded up all books, so that you alone hold the teacher's chair. You have taken away all prophets, so that you alone are to be questioned about the mysteries of God. You have destroyed all learning, so that for everything, you alone have the answer.

And so, O love, our mother, O beauty and life of the virtues, all virtue draws from you the power to be truly virtue, from you it borrows garment and life. Every virtue is naked without you, having no garment in which to clothe itself. Even if it has something, unless it is gilded by you, it is in no way a wedding garment. Furthermore every virtue is not only deformed without you, having no charm or beauty, but since it lacks you, its form, it is obviously unformed and empty. If it does not draw its life from you, it is more than languid, it is lifeless. All virtues that are not quickened by you can have indeed the appearance of virtue but not the reality.

It is you who have the right to say: 'Wisdom is mine, and sound judgment; discretion is mine, and fortitude'. In a word, all things are yours, for you are Christ's. You are the true wisdom which reaches from end to end mightily, for you are the blessed end of all perfection; here the end of all justice, there the end of all glory.

John of Forde[15]

Love is reciprocal; it is shared by God and the soul.

Love in us mounts up to you, O Lord,
because the love in you comes down to us.
You loved us,
you came down to us;
by loving you we shall mount up to you.

William of Saint Thierry[16]

Let no one who loves God have any doubt that God loves him. The love of God for us precedes our love for him and it also follows it. How could he be reluctant to love us in return for our love when he loved us even when we did not love him? I say he loved us. As a pledge of his love you have the Spirit, and you have a faithful witness to it in Jesus, Jesus crucified. A double and irrefutable argument of God's love for us.

Christ died and so deserved our love.
The Holy Spirit works upon us and makes us love him.
Christ has given us a reason for loving himself,
the Spirit the power to love him.
The one commends his great
love to us, the other gives it.
In the one we see the object of our love,
by the other we have the power to love.
The former provides the occasion for our
love, the latter provides the love itself.

How shameful it would be to look with ungrateful eyes upon the Son of God dying for us? But this could easily be were the Spirit lacking. 'The charity of God is poured forth in our hearts by the Holy Spirit who is given to us'. Loved, we love in return, and loving, we deserve to be still more loved. If while we were still his enemies we were reconciled to God by the death of his Son, how much more being reconciled shall we be saved through his life. Why so? 'He that spared not even his own Son, but delivered him up for us all, how has he not also, with him, given us all things?'

Bernard of Clairvaux[17]

You first loved us so that we might love you.
And that was not because you needed to be loved by us,
but because we could not be what you created us to be,
except by loving you.
Having then in many ways
and on various occasions
spoken to the fathers by the prophets,
now in these last days you have
spoken to us in the Son, your Word.
For you to speak thus in your
Son was an open declaration
of how much and in what sort of way you loved us,
in that you spared not your own Son,
but delivered him up for us all.
And he himself loved us and gave himself for us.

William of Saint Thierry[18]

*This mutual love—God's love within us and our
love for God—is the Holy Spirit of God, working
within us.*

This outpouring of love into our expanded hearts is effected by the love of God—the love, that is, of the Father for the Son; it is effected through the Holy Spirit who is given to us—who is himself the love of the Father and the Son and their mutual union.

Baldwin of Forde[19]

The Holy Spirit is the almighty Artificer who creates man's good will in regard to God, inclines God to be merciful to us, shapes our desire, gives strength, ensures the prosperity of undertakings, conducts all things powerfully and disposes everything sweetly. He it is who gives life to our spirit and holds it together, just as it gives life to its body and holds it together. Other people may teach us how to seek God, and angels, how to adore him, but the Holy Spirit alone teaches how to find him, possess him and enjoy him. The Spirit himself is the anxious quest of the one who truly seeks, he is the devotion of the one who adores in spirit and truth, he is the wisdom of the one who finds, the love of the one who possesses, the gladness of the one who enjoys.

William of Saint Thierry[20]

Grant me to love you with all my heart,
to cling to you with all my soul,
to expend all my force in your love and service,
to live after your own heart;
and,
being prepared by you,
to go, at the hour of death, spotless into your nuptials.

Gertrud of Helfta[21]

Sources and Scriptural References

1. *The Mirror of Charity* 1.16.49; CF 17:114.
   Mt 22:40.
2. *Tractate* 15; CF 41:159.
3. *On the Song of Songs* 64.10; CF 31:177.
   Phil 2:7.
4. *Sermon* 19.2; CF 20:239–240.

5. *On the Song of Songs* 20.4; CF 4:150.
   Dt 6:5; Sg 8:6.
6. Tractate 15; CF 41:173–174.
   Mt 22:37; Ws 6:16; Is 33:6.
7. Sermon 31.21; CF 66.
8. Tractate 13; CF 41:135–136.
   Jn 12:32; Sg 1:3; Ps 84:11; 1 Cor 13:8.
9. *The Mirror of Charity* 1.28.80; CF 17:135.
10. *The Nature and Dignity of Love* 21; CF 30:77–78, excerpted.
11. Tractate 13; CF 41:135–136.
    Jn 12:32; Sg 1:3; Ps 84:11; 1 Cor 13:8.
12. Sermon 16.15; CF 11:134–135.
    Jn 17:3; Jn 15:1; Jn 14:6.
13. *On Contemplating God* 11; CF 3:56.
14. *On the Song of Songs* 83.4; CF 40:184.
15. *Sermon* 12.7; CF 29:225–226.
    Ps 45:10; Prov 8:14; 1 Cor 3:23; Ws 8:1.
16. *Meditation* 6.4; CF 3:126–127.
17. Letter 107.8 (B.S. James trans. 109.8); CF 62:162–163.
    Rv 1:5; 1 Cor 2:2; Rom 5:8, 5, 10; Rom 8:32;
18. *On Contemplating God* 10; CF 3:52.
    1 Jn 4:10; Heb 1:2; Rom 8:32; Gal 2:20.
19. *Tractate* 13; CF 41:136.
20. *The Golden Epistle* 265; CF 12:96.
21. *Spiritual Exercise* 2; CF 49:37.

10 ❧

The Blessedness of Love

'Blessed are the pure in heart, for they shall see God', the Lord says in the fifth chapter of the Gospel according to Matthew. The Cistercians, who longed with all their being to see God, interpreted the Beatitudes in the Gospel as steps to God, who is Love.

*T*HE BEATITUDES are a happy beginning, full of the new grace of the new dispensation. No matter how lacking in faith a person may be, or how reluctant to respond, he will be almost compelled to give his attention and even more to act when he hears blessedness being promised to the wretched and the kingdom of heaven to those in exile or in want.

This, I say, is a happy beginning of the new law, full of promise. From the very first, the Lawgiver confers the manifold blessing of these beatitudes on the human race which is thereby attracted to progress from virtue to virtue by climbing these eight steps which the structure of this Gospel ladder has set in our hearts according to the model of the heavenly image, the model which was shown to Ezekiel on the mountain of the visions of God. In this arrangement of the virtues in a series of eight steps there can clearly be seen a certain stairway for the heart and a progression in merits. We are led step by step from the lowest states of evangelical perfection to the very highest until we enter the temple on Sion and behold the God of gods. It was in reference to this temple that the Prophet speaks: 'And the ascent to it was by eight steps'.

The first virtue in this ascent, proper to beginners, is renunciation of the world, which makes us poor in spirit. The second is meekness, which enables us to submit ourselves in obedience and to accustom ourselves to such submission. Next comes mourning to make us weep for our sins and to beg God for virtue. It is here that we first taste justice, and so learn to hunger and thirst more keenly after justice in ourselves as well as in others, and we begin to be roused to zeal against sinful men. Then, lest this zeal should grow immoderate and lead to vice, mercy follows to temper it. When a person has learned to become merciful and just by diligent practice of these virtues he will then perhaps be fit to enter upon the way of contemplation and to give himself to the task of obtaining that purity of heart which will enable him to see God. Tested and proved in this way in both the active and the contemplative life, he who bears the name and office of a son of God through his having become the servant of others will then and only then be worthy to be a peacemaker between them and God. Thus he will fulfill the office of mediator and advocate, and be worthy to make peace. If a person is faithful and constant in this office, he will often attain that virtue and merit which belong to the martyr, for he suffers persecution for justice's sake.

Guerric of Igny[1]

The wisdom of God and the wisdom of this world judge the value of things in different ways, and when they weigh in the balance the importance of things, they do not use the same standard. Things which the wisdom of God counts worthy of rejection and contempt are held by the wisdom of the world to be of great value, and the wisdom of the world rejects in its own judgment the things which the wisdom of God judges to be great and precious.

The wisdom of God says, 'Blessed are the poor in spirit, for theirs is the kingdom of Heaven'. The wisdom of the world says, 'Blessed are the rich, for now they have dominion in all the world'. The wisdom of God says, 'Blessed are those who mourn, for they shall be comforted'. The wisdom of the world says, 'Blessed are those who laugh, for even now they are comforted'. The wisdom of the world approves and praises and loves the riches and laughter and joy of this present life, for they provide present comfort; it hates and despises poverty and grief, for in them is present desolation. The wisdom of God judges the joys of this present life to be vain and harmful, for our vices feed on them and they are stumbling-blocks to salvation. But poverty and grief it commends and loves, for they purge our vices and are a preparation for endless bliss.

In this way, the wisdom of God and the wisdom of this world attack each other in their judgments. Each judges the other in turn, and each in turn is judged. The wisdom of this world is foolishness with God, and the wisdom of God is foolishness with the world. To those that perish, the word of the cross is foolishness, but in a certain way, the word of the cross is the word of poverty and grief, for poverty or grief is a sort of cross. The wisdom of God is justified by her children and the children of light, but the children of this world are wiser in their generation than the children of light. The children of this world, therefore, and the children of light reckon each other to be foolish and insane! The latter look to vanities and lying follies; the former love to have as their light the foolishness of the preaching. It is through this preaching that God determined that those who believe should be saved, and it is this which the sensual person does not comprehend. It is foolishness to him, and he cannot understand.

Baldwin of Forde[2]

Blessed are the poor in spirit, for theirs is the kingdom of heaven:

The true Word of the Father speaks that which he is, divine Wisdom teaches what he is and says: 'Happy are the poor in spirit'. Wisely indeed he puts first, giving it precedence over everything else, what everyone seeks, everyone craves and desires, though almost all go astray in their search for it.

For who does not want to be happy? Why do people universally quarrel and fight, bargain, resort to flattery, and inflict injuries on one another? Is it not simply in order to obtain, by fair means or foul, what seems good to them, something that promises to make them happy? For everyone imagines himself the happier the more he obtains what he desires.

We agree, then, in our desire for happiness, but our conceptions of it differ widely. For one it consists in physical pleasure and fleeting enjoyment, for another in strength of character, for yet another in knowledge of truth.

So the Teacher of all men, who by love alone has become a debtor to the unwise as well as to the wise, begins by redirecting those who have lost the way, then he gives guidance to those who are making good progress, and finally he gives admittance to those knocking at the door, just as he says: 'Knock and the door will be opened to you'. In the name of the wanderers the Prophet prays: 'Guide me, Lord, in your way'; for those on the way: 'Let me walk in your truth'; for those who are knocking: 'Make my heart rejoice to reverence your name'. And in another psalm again he prays for the wanderers: 'Lead me, Lord, in your justice'; for those on the journey: 'Make my path straight in your sight'; and for those who are knocking: 'May all those that trust in you have joy, they will rejoice for ever and you will dwell in them; all those that love your name will glory in you'.

So he who is the Way, the Truth and the Life, he who corrects, guides and welcomes, begins with the words: 'Happy are the poor in spirit'. The false wisdom of this world, which is true stupidity, not understanding what it is saying nor of what it is speaking, has its own scale of values. In its estimation the happy are those aliens whose right hand is the right hand of falsehood and whose mouth speaks lies, because their barns are full to overflowing, their flocks are increasing and their cattle fat. In a word, they have everything that relates to wealth that may fail, and to peace that is no peace, and to empty gladness. In direct contradiction, the Wisdom of God, the Right Hand of the Father, his own Son, the Mouth that speaks truth, declares that the happy people are the poor, they will be the kings of a kingdom that is everlasting.

As if he were to say: 'You seek happiness but it is not where you think it is. You are running hard, but off the track. Here is the right road, here is the way to happiness. Poverty is the way, poverty willingly embraced for my sake. Happiness is the kingdom of heaven in me. You run energetically but not profitably, for the faster you run, the further you are from the track. Poverty is the way to happiness. Keep to the way and you will arrive'.

Courage, then; it is for us to listen to the Poor Man commending poverty to the poor. Someone speaking from experience is to be believed; Christ was born poor, lived poor and died poor. He willed to die; certainly he did not will to become rich. Let us believe Truth when he tells us of the way to life. If it is hard, it is brief, while happiness is eternal. It is narrow but it leads to life and brings us out into freedom; it will set our feet in an open place. It is steep, of course it is, for it goes uphill, it reaches to heaven! So we must be lightly equipped, not heavily encumbered, for the climb.

What are we seeking? Is it happiness? The Truth shows us true happiness. Is it wealth? The king shares his kingdom and makes kings. Human beings are plagued with a restless desire for novelty. Though they can obtain a sufficiency without difficulty, they must sweat for more. Some make five yoke of oxen a pretext for not coming to the heavenly wedding feast, the feast in which poverty becomes plenitude, want becomes satiety, and the last place becomes the first. There lowliness is transformed into greatness and labor into repose. Elisha slaughtered

just such oxen that he might follow Elijah the more readily. Taking this as model and type, let us follow Christ.

Isaac of Stella[3]

*Blessed are the meek, for they shall inherit the
earth:*

It is meekness which gives one a gentle and calm manner
towards others; compunction that makes one watchful
and faithful; justice that gives one a certain refinement
and perfection both within and without, while mercy
urges one to do good to many and to wish well to all.
By one's love of poverty he spurns the laughing world;
with the strength of his meekness he despises its anger;
through the gift of compunction he regains himself; in
striving for justice he surrenders himself to God, and
with mercy he gains his neighbor. Because of his love
for poverty he is content with little; in his habitual gentleness he is troublesome to none; his deep compunction
makes him alert to himself; in the firmness of his justice
he is acceptable to God and in the sweetness of his mercy
he is all things to all men.

Isaac of Stella[4]

*Blessed are those who mourn, for they shall be
comforted:*

One must mourn greatly; but with deeply-felt piety and
ensuing comfort. Let him consider that within himself
he will find no rest for himself, because he is full of

misery and desolation. Let him consider that there is no good in his flesh and that the present evil age contains nothing but vanity and affliction of spirit. Let him consider, I repeat, that he will find no comfort—not within nor under nor around himself, until he at last learns to seek it from above and to hope that it will come down from above. Meanwhile let him mourn and lament his sorrow, let his eyes well with tears and his eyelids find no slumber. Tears will wash the darkness from his eyes, his sight will become keen so he will be able to turn his gaze towards the brightness of glistening light.

Bernard of Clairvaux[5]

Blessed are those who hunger and thirst for righteousness; they shall be satisfied:

Who are the hungry who are filled with good things, and who thereby are truly and fully satisfied? Who but those of whom it is written, 'Blessed are those who hunger and thirst for righteousness'! And what is this righteousness which satisfies us and makes us blessed but Christ, whom God made our wisdom and our righteousness? He indeed is Wisdom who says, 'Those who eat me shall still hunger, and those who drink me shall still thirst'. Christ was made our righteousness, justifying us freely, freely distributing righteousness, and through righteousness remaining in us, the giver of the gift with the gift. Our food is he who bestows righteousness, and our food is also the righteousness he bestows.

Baldwin of Forde[6]

Is there someone among you, brothers, who desires to be satisfied and would like this desire to be fulfilled?

Then let him begin to be hungry for righteousness, and he cannot fail to be satisfied. Let him yearn for those loaves which abound in his father's house, and he will immediately find he is disgusted with the husks of swine. Let him endeavor, however little, to experience the taste of righteousness that he may desire it more and thus merit more; as it has been written: 'He who eats me will hunger for more, and he who drinks me will thirst for more.' This desire is more akin to the spirit, and because it is natural to it, the heart is more eagerly preoccupied with this and manfully shoves out all other desires. In this way a strong man fully armed is overcome by one stronger than he; in this way one nail is driven out by another.

Blessed are they who hunger and thirst for righteousness, then, for they will be satisfied. Not yet by that one thing by which a person is never sated, the one thing by which he lives, but by everything else, all those things for which he previously longed insatiably, so that thereafter the will ceases delivering up the body to obey its former passions, and delivers it over to reason, urging it to serve righteousness for holiness' sake with no less zeal than it formerly showed in serving evil for iniquity's.

Bernard of Clairvaux[7]

Blessed are the merciful, for they shall obtain mercy:

If you want God to be merciful to you, then, you must yourself be merciful towards your soul. Flood your bed every night with your tears, remember to drench your couch with your weeping. If you have compassion on yourself, if you struggle on in groanings of penance—for this is mercy's first step—then you will arrive at mercy. And if you are perhaps a great and frequent sinner and seek great mercy and frequent forgiveness, you must also work at increasing your mercy. You are reconciled to yourself whereas you had become a burden to yourself, because you had set yourself up against God. Once peace has been restored this way in your own house, the first thing to do is to extend it to your neighbors so that God may come at last to kiss you with the very kiss of his mouth. In this way being reconciled to God, as it has been written, you may have peace. Forgive those who have sinned against you, and you will be forgiven your sins when you pray to the Father with an easy conscience and say: forgive us our trespasses, as we forgive those who trespass against us.

Bernard of Clairvaux[8]

Blessed are the pure of heart, for they shall see God:

A heart that would contemplate must be bright as a mirror, shimmer like some still stretch of water crystal-clear, so that in it and through it the mind may see itself, as in and through a mirror, an image in the image of God. The heart that covets the sight of God as in a mirror must keep itself free from cares, from harmful, unnecessary and even necessary ones. It must keep itself ever alert through reading, meditation and prayer. Blessed are the pure of heart; they shall see God. May he grant that we do so. Amen.

Isaac of Stella[9]

*Blessed are the peacemakers, for they shall be
called sons of God:*

A peaceful person repays good for good, as far as in him
lies, and wishes harm to no one. Someone else may be
patient and repay no one evil for evil, being even able
to bear with the one who hurts him. There is also the
peacemaker: he is always ready to repay good for evil
and to help the one who hurts him.

The first is one of those little ones who is easily scandal-
ized; for him it will not be easy to win salvation in this
present evil age so full of stumbling blocks. The second
possesses his soul in patience, as has been written. As for
the third, he not only possesses his own soul, but wins
many more.

The first, as far as he is able, is in peace. The second keeps
peace. The third makes peace. Appropriately therefore
is he blessed with the name son, for he accomplishes
the duty incumbent on the son: that once he has himself
been acceptably reconciled, he in turn reconciles others
to his Father. Now someone who serves well gains good
standing for himself, and what better standing could
there be in the father's house than that of the son? For,
'if sons, then heirs, heirs of God and fellow heirs with
Christ.'

Bernard of Clairvaux[10]

Last of all, the Lord our God has blessed his people—and
we are that people—with peace, and not with one kind of
peace but with two. There is the peace we have among
ourselves and from ourselves to everyone, and there is

the peace we have with God. It is our duty carefully to guard both kinds of peace, and to put them to good use with real earnestness. We must see to it that we take away even the least stone that might make us stumble on the road of peace where, by the mercy of God, we are walking, and each one of us must take all possible measures, as the apostle says, to please his brother so as to edify him. In this peace, our designs and desires find their joyful perfection, so that the peace of Christ exults in our hearts, and peace is perfected by peace, and we take our delight in the great, satisfying richness of our present peace.

Blessed be the Lord our God, who has blessed us with manifold blessings, and day by day extends these blessings and makes them more glorious.

John of Forde[11]

Sources and Scriptural References

1. Sermon 53.1–2; CF 32:204–206.
   Mt 5:4–11; Ps 84:8; Heb 8:5; Ez 40:31.
2. Tractate 9.3; CF 41:47–48.
   1 Cor 3:18–19; Lk 7:35; Lk 16:8; Ps 40:5; 1 Cor 1:21; 1 Cor 2:14.
3. Sermon 1.14–20; CF 11:7–9.
   Mt 5:2; Rom 1:14; Lk 11:9; Ps 86:11; Ps 5:9; Jn 14:6; Ps 144:8–14; Ps 31:9; Lk 14:19; 1 K 19:19.
4. Sermon 3.20; CF 11:26–27.
   Mt 5:5; 1 Cor 9:22.
5. *Sermon on Conversion* 23; CF 25:57–58.
   Mt 5:4; Lk 11:21; Ps 38:3; Gal 1:4; Qo 1:14; Col 3:1; Jb 10:20; Ps 119:136; Jb 16:17; Acts 22:11.

6. *Tractate* 9.4; CF 41:68.
   Mt 5:6; 1 Cor 1:30; Si 24:29.
7. *Sermon on Conversion* 27; CF 25:62–63.
   Mt 5:6; Lk 15:16; Si 24:29; Lk 11:21–22; Rom 6:12, 19.
8. *Sermon on Conversion* 29; CF 25:65–66.
   Mt 5:7; Ps 6:6; Ps 51:1; Jb 7:20; Sg 1:1; Rom 5:10, 1; Mt 6:12.
9. Sermon 25.15; CF 11:209.
   Mt 5:8; 1 Cor 13:12; 2 Cor 3:18.
10. *Sermon on Conversion* 31; CF 25:68.
    Mt 5:9; Rom 12:17; Mk 9:41; Gal 1:4; Lk 21:19; 1 Cor 9:19;
    2 Cor 5:18; 1 Tm 3:13; Rom 8:17.
11. Sermon 18.9–10; CF 39:58–59.
    Mt 5:9; Ps 29:11; Rom 15:2; Col 3:15.

11 ～

The Fullness of Love

*In this school of love there is always more to be
learned. Love is infinite. Someone who has made
progress in this school can be sure that it is*

love that has drawn her and led her and taught her
the ways that she has faithfully followed. Often in great
labor and in many activities, in great infirmity and in
strong desire, in frequent impatience and in great dis-
satisfaction, in adversity and in prosperity, in great pain,
in seeking and asking, in lacking and in having, in
climbing and in hanging suspended, in following and
in striving, in need and anxiety, in fear and concern,
in great faithfulness and in many unfaithfulnesses, in
pleasure and in pain, is she ready to suffer. In death and
in life she commits herself to love.

Beatrice of Nazareth[1]

*She need have no hesitation in desiring an ever-
deeper union with the God who is infinite love.*

Once you have had the experience of God's benevolence,
you need no longer feel abashed in aspiring to a holier in-
timacy. Growth in grace brings expansion of confidence.

You will love with greater ardor, and knock on the door with greater assurance, in order to gain what you perceive to be still wanting to you. 'The one who knocks will always have the door opened to him'. It is my belief that to a person so disposed, God will not refuse that most intimate kiss of all, a mystery of supreme generosity and ineffable sweetness.

Bernard of Clairvaux[2]

When our Lord's bride has come further and ascends higher into greater piety, she feels another mode of love in a closer understanding and a higher knowledge. She feels that love has overcome all her opponents within her and has made good her defects. Love has mastered her knowing and allowed her to receive the free disposal over herself without opposition so that she holds her heart in safety, she experiences it in rest and she does what is to be done in freedom.

Beatrice of Nazareth[3]

This union, this deeper understanding, is the flowering of the search for God.

It is enchanting enough to seek you, good Jesus,
but more enchanting to hold you.
The former is a devout task,
the latter sheer joy.
To embrace you is surely enchanting,
for your very touch is rewarding.

Gilbert of Hoyland[4]

'I found him, I held him and I will not let him go'. 'I found him' by yearning for him, 'I held him' by dwelling on him in my memory, and 'I will not let go' by uninterrupted recollection. 'I held him'. When you also have found Christ, when you have found wisdom, when you have found justice, holiness and redemption (for Christ became all these for us), when you have found all these, hold them by affection and by attention. What you have found by understanding, hold by diligence and keep hold, if I may so express it, of the elusive virtues. Clasp their slippery forms to you in a tighter embrace until, reversing their roles, they cling to you, embrace you willingly, hold you fast without the labor of your own initiative, and permit you neither to depart very far nor to be away very long. Even if at times you should turn aside to meet the claims of human need, there let them pursue you, recall you, and clutch you to themselves, so that if they cannot always have your uninterrupted attention, they may always have your dedicated affection.

Gilbert of Hoyland[5]

Love experienced becomes 'a communion of wills and an agreement in charity'.[6]

Holy and chaste,
full of sweetness and delight,
love utterly serene and true,
mutual and deep,
which joins two beings,
not in one flesh but in one spirit,
making them no longer two but one.

As Paul says:
'Someone who is united to God
is one spirit with him'.

Bernard of Clarivaux[7]

No longer does the will merely desire what God desires, not only does it love him, but it is perfect in its love, so that it can will only what God wills. Now to will what God wills is already to be like God, to be able to will only what God wills is already to be what God is; for him to will and to be are the same thing. Therefore it is well said that we shall see him fully as he is when we are like him, that is, when we are what he is. For those who have been enabled to become children of God have been enabled to become, not indeed God, but what God is: holy—and in the future, fully happy as God is. And the source of their present holiness and their future happiness is none other than God himself who is at once their holiness and their happiness . . . This makes a person one with God, one spirit, not only with the unity which comes of willing the same thing but with a greater fullness of virtue, as has been said: the inability to will anything else.

It is called 'unity of spirit', not only because the Holy Spirit brings it about or inclines a man's spirit to it, but because it is the Holy Spirit himself, the God who is Charity, who is the Love of Father and Son, their Unity, Sweetness, Good, Kiss Embrace and whatever else they have in common in that supreme unity of truth and truth of unity.

William of Saint Thierry[8]

*This unity is something greatly to be desired, to
be prayed for.*

This is the goal for which the solitary strives, this is the
end he has in view, this is his reward, the rest that comes
after his labors, the consolation for his pains: and this is
the perfection and the true wisdom of man. It embraces
within itself and contains all the virtues, and they are not
borrowed from another source but as it were naturally
implanted in it, so that it resembles God who is himself
whatever he is.

William of Saint Thierry[9]

Lead me away, my refuge and my strength, into the
heart of the desert as once you led your servant Moses;
lead me where the bush burns, yet is not burnt up,
where the holy soul that has earned admission to a like
experience is all aflame with the fullness of the fire of
your Holy Spirit, and, burning like the seraphim, is not
consumed but cleansed. And then there comes to pass
for the first time a better thing, the miracle of all your
miracles, the sight of sights. The soul attains to the holy
place where none may stand or take another step, except
she be bare-footed—having loosed the shoestrings of all
fleshly hindrances—the place, that is, that the soul may
enter only with her affections clean and pure. This is
the place where He Who Is, who cannot be seen as he
is, is notwithstanding heard to say, 'I Am Who Am', the
place where, for the time, the soul must cover her face so
that she does not see the face of God, and yet in humble
obedience must use her ears to hear what the Lord God
will say concerning her.

William of Saint Thierry[10]

This is a place of deep peace and stillness.

There is a place where God is seen in tranquil rest, where he is neither Judge nor Teacher but Bridegroom. There one clearly realizes that 'the Lord's love for those who fear him lasts forever and forever'. It is there that one may happily say: 'I am a friend to all who fear you and observe your precepts'. God's purpose stands fast, the peace he has planned for those who fear him is without recall.

O place so truly quiet, where God is not encountered in angry guise nor distracted as it were by cares, but where his will is proved good and desirable and perfect. This is a vision that charms rather than terrifies; that does not arouse an inquisitive restlessness, but restrains it; that calms rather than wearies the senses. Here one may indeed be at rest. The God of peace pacifies all things, and to gaze on this stillness is to find repose. There he wills to be found in the guise of love, calm and peaceful, gracious and meek, filled with mercy for all who gaze on him.

Bernard of Clairvaux[11]

Be still now;
taste and see how sweet and
how remarkable is the spouse
whom you have chosen above thousands.
See what and how great is that glory
for which you have forsaken the world.
See what that good is like for which you have waited.
See what the homeland is like
for which you have sighed.

See what the prize is like for which you have labored.
See who your God is,
what he is like and how great he is,
whom you have cherished,
whom you have adored
and for whom you have always wished.

Gertrud of Helfta[12]

*It is a place where the soul is rapt by God, where
the language of human love must be used, yet
must be understood as being itself a reflection
of infinite divine love.*

The beauty of love devours her.
The power of love consumes her.
The sweetness of love drowns her.
The greatness of love absorbs her.
The nobility of love holds her.
The purity of love adorns her.
The height of love has drawn
her upwards and makes her one.
So she must exist totally for love
and is unable to love anything else.

Beatrice of Nazareth[13]

Lord, whither do you draw those whom you thus em-
brace and enfold, save to your heart? The manna of your
Godhead, which you, O Jesus, keep within the golden
vessel of your all-wise human soul, is your sweet heart!
Blessed are they whom your embrace draws close to it.
Blessed the souls whom you have hidden in your heart,

that inmost hiding-place, so that your arms overshadow them from the disquieting of men and they only hope in your covering and fostering wings. Those who are hidden in your secret heart are overshadowed by your mighty arms; they sleep sweetly, and look forward joyfully, for they share the merit of a good conscience and the anticipation of your promised reward.

William of Saint Thierry[14]

Sources and Scriptural References

1. 528; *The Seven Modes of Love*, Tjurunga No. 50, 82.
   Cf. CF 50:329.
2. *On the Song of Songs* 3.5; CF 4:19.
   Lk 11:10.
3. 312; *The Seven Modes of Love*, Tjurunga No. 50, 78. CF 50 ref?
4. Sermon 1.2; CF 14:45.
5. Sermon 9.2; CF 14:129.
   Sg 3:4; 1 Cor 1:30.
6. Bernard of Clairvaux, *On the Song of Songs* 71.10; CF 40:56.
7. *On the Song of Songs* 83.6; CF 40:186.
   Mt 19:5; 1 Cor 6:17.
8. *The Golden Epistle* 257–258, 262–263; CF 12:94–96.
   1 Cor 6:17; 1 Jn 3:2; Jn 1:12.
9. *The Golden Epistle* 276; CF 12:99.
10. *Meditation* 4.10; CF 3.116.
    Ps 46:2; Ex 3:1–14; Ps 85:9.
11. *On the Song of Songs* 23.15–16; CF 7:38–40.
    Ps 103:17; Ps 119:63; Rom 12:2; Ps 86:5.
12. Spiritual Exercise 6; CF 49:95–96.
    Ps 46:10; Ps 34:8.
13. 196; *The Seven Modes of Love*, Tjurunga No. 50, 75.
    Cf. CF 50:305.
14. *Meditation* 8.4; CF 3:141.
    Heb 9:4; Ps 40:9; Ps 31:22; Ps 91:4; Ps 17:8.

12 ∾

The Perfection of Love

The final perfection of love comes not in this world, but in God's presence; here we await it in the life to come.

O UR REWARD LIES with God
who was the source of the gift of our being.
He is beginning and end to us:
the beginning to whom we come at last,
the end that holds the primacy of importance;
perfect beginning because of the end,
infinite end because ever beginning.

Isaac of Stella[1]

What can we do but yearn for that place of rest, of security, of exultation, of wonder, of overwhelming joy?

Bernard of Clairvaux[2]

Here we desire God. There desire will become fruition. Here we believe. There vision will take the place of faith.

In heaven one vision is offered to everyone who sees. For as he who is seen is immutable in himself, he is present immutably to all who contemplate him; to these there is nothing more desirable that they wish to see, nothing more enticing that they could see. Can their eager appetite, then, ever grow weary, or that sweetness ebb away, or that truth prove deceptive, or that eternity come to a close? And if both the ability and will to contemplate are prolonged eternally, what is lacking to total happiness? Those who contemplate him without ceasing are short of nothing, those whose wills are fixed on him have nothing more to desire.

Bernard of Clairvaux[3]

O you righteous, rejoice and exult, because you see him whom you love, you have him whom you have long desired, you hold him whom you never fear to lose. Therefore, sing and exult in him, for he is the Lord your God, glorious and beautiful, he is salvation and life, honor and glory, peace and all good things. How great a peace is there, where nothing annoys you whether from others or from yourselves, but the Lord is your shepherd and you lack nothing. He has prepared for you a kingdom, that you may eat and drink at his table in his kingdom. 'Taste then and see how sweet the Lord is'.[4]

The fruit we must expect as our love's fulfillment should be worthy of the promise of him whom we love: 'A full measure, pressed down, shaken together and running over, will be poured into your lap'. And that measure, as I have heard, will be without measure.

But what is the nature of that which is to be measured out, what that immense reward is which has been promised? The eye has not seen, O God, besides you, what things you have prepared for them that love you. Tell us then, since you do the preparing, tell us what it is you prepare. We believe, we are confident, that in accordance with your promise, 'we shall be filled with the good things of your house'.

But—I persist in asking—what are these good things, what are they like? Would it be with corn and wine and oil, with gold and silver or precious stones? But these are things that we have known and seen, that we have grown weary of seeing. We seek for the things that no eye has seen and no ear has heard, things beyond the mind of man. To search after these things, whatever they may be, is a source of pleasure and relish and delight. 'They will all be taught by God', says Scripture, and 'he will be all in all'. As I see it, the fullness that we hope for from God will be only something of God himself.

Who indeed can comprehend what an abundance of goodness is contained in that brief expression: 'God will be all in all'? He who satisfies with good the desire of the soul will one day himself be for the reason fullness of light, for the will, the fullness of peace, for the memory, eternity's uninterrupted flow.

When error will have gone from the reason, pain from the will, and every trace of fear from the memory, then will come that state for which we hope, with its admirable serenity, its fullness of delight, its endless security. The God who is truth is the source of the first of these gifts; the God who is love, of the second; the God who is all-powerful, of the third.

And so it will come to pass that God will be all in all, for the reason will receive unquenchable light, the will imperturbable peace, the memory an unfailing fountain from which it will draw eternally.

Bernard of Clairvaux[5]

Fountain of sempiternal light,
fetch me back into the flow of your abyss
from which I flowed forth—
there where I may recognize
you just as I am recognized,
and love you just as I am loved—
so that forever I may see you,
my God,
as you really are
in your blessed vision, fruition, and possession. Amen.

Gertrud of Helfta[6]

There the soul is united to its bridegroom, and is wholly made one spirit with him in inseparable faithfulness and eternal love. Having worshiped him in the time of grace, it will have fruition of him in eternal glory where there will be no activity save praising and loving. May God lead us all there. Amen.

Beatrice of Nazareth[7]

Sources and Scriptural References

1. Sermon 25.8; CF 11:207.
   Rv 1:8.
2. *On the Song of Songs* 33.2; CF 7:145.
3. *On the Song of Songs* 31.1; CF 7:125.
4. 'The Spirit and the Soul', in *Three Treatises on Man* CF 24:272–273.
   Ps 33:1; Ps 23:1; Lk 22:29; Ps 34:9.
5. *On the Song of Songs* 11.4–6; CF 4.72–74.
   Lk 6:38; Jn 3:34; Is 64:4; Ps 65:5; Ps 4:8; 1 Cor 2:9; Jn 6:45; 1 Cor 15:28; Ps 31:20; Ps 103:5.
6. Spiritual Exercise 5; CF 49.83.
   1 Jn 3:2.
7. *The Seven Degrees of Love* 262; CF 50:331.

Biographical Notes

Aelred of Rievaulx

Aelred came from Hexham, in northern England, and was educated at Durham. As a young man, he lived at the scottish royal court. He entered the monastery of Rievaulx in 1134, and became successively novice master there, then first abbot of Revesby, its daughter house. In 1147 he was elected abbot of Rievaulx, a post he retained, in spite of increasing ill-health, until his death. Blessed with a radiant and sympathetic personality, he had a gift for friendship and a talent for guiding his monks with gentleness and wisdom.

Aelred's first work, undertaken at the urging of Bernard, was *The Mirror of Charity*. In it he describes the ties joining the love of self, neighbor, and God. His later writings include a meditation on *Jesus at the Age of Twelve* and a *Rule for a Recluse* , both of which reveal his devotion to the humanity of Christ. In his best known work, *On Spiritual Friendship*, he explains how human friendship becomes a path to God.

Baldwin of Forde

The details of Baldwin's early life are uncertain. He came probably from Exeter in Devonshire, England; he may have studied law in Italy. In 1150 he was appointed tutor to the nephew of Pope Innocent II. In 1161 he was made archdeacon of the cathedral at Exeter. After the martyrdom of Thomas Becket, and perhaps influenced by it, Baldwin entered the nearby monastery of Ford (or Forde) in Dorset. In 1175 he was elected abbot. Most of his *Spiritual Tractates* incorporate sermons to his monks and date from this period. While treating a variety of subjects, Baldwin never loses sight of the centrality of love, and reflects particularly the communion among the three persons of the Trinity, the basis of our communion with God and with one another.

Baldwin's monastic years were probably the happiest and most fruitful of his life. He went on to become bishop of Worcester, and then archbishop of Canterbury. In 1190 he went on crusade to the Holy Land, where he died during the siege of Acre, disillusioned and saddened by the conduct of the crusaders.

Beatrice of Nazareth

The thirteenth century saw a great spiritual vitality among women, particularly in the Low Countries. Beatrice was both part of this current and in continuity with cistercian spirituality of the previous century. After her mother died when she was seven, her father sent her to be educated by a group of religious women. Three years later, he took her and her two sisters to Florival, a house of cistercian nuns which he himself had helped found. Six years after that, the three sisters made profession as Cistercians, while their father and brother became lay brothers attached to the monastery. The whole family later moved to the monastery of Maagdendaal, and finally, in 1236, to a new foundation at Nazareth, where Beatrice held the position of prioress until her death in 1268.

From an early age, Beatrice kept notes of her ascetical practices and spiritual experiences. Parts of these were incorporated into her biography, as was her *Seven Modes of Love*, in which she describes, with her own special verve, not so much the soul's ascent to God, as different aspects of the experience of love.

Bernard of Clairvaux

The best known of the early Cistercians, Bernard was born in 1090 in Burgundy, France, and there he received his early education. When, at the age of twenty, he decided to enter the obscure monastery of Cîteaux, he persuaded his brothers, relatives, and friends—thirty of them—to accompany him. Three years later he was sent at the head of a group of monks to found the abbey of Clairvaux, where he remained abbot until his death in 1153. He attracted so many men to Clairvaux that during his lifetime sixty foundations were made from it. As his reputation grew, he was called upon to advise bishops, nobles, nuns, scholars, kings, and popes, and to settle disputes in both Church and 'the world'. Yet he remained above all a man dedicated to God and zealous for leading others to God. Down the ages, through his writings he has continued to be what he was for Dante: an incomparable teacher and guide to the heights of contemplative prayer.

His early works, *The Steps of Humility and Pride*, *On Loving God*, and *On Grace and Free Choice*—all written at the request of others—established the basis of his teaching. His masterpiece is his commentary *On the Song of Songs*, in which, in eighty-six sermons, he treats many aspects of the spiritual and mystical life. Begun in 1135, the series had reached only Chapter 3, verse 1, of the *Song of Songs* by the time of his death. Among his numerous other writings are *Sermons for the Seasons and Feasts of the Year*, *Occasional Sermons*, and *Sermons on Conversion*. In *Five Books on Consideration*, written for one of his former monks who had been raised to the papal throne, Bernard invites his reader to consider what lies below, around and above them. A collection of Bernard's *Letters* gives us insights into his charismatic personality and manifold activities.

Getrud of Helfta

At the age of five Gertrud was taken to the convent of Helfta, in german Saxony, a house which followed cistercian customs without being juridically attached to the Order. There she received a good education in the liberal arts. At the age of twenty-five she experienced an encounter with Christ which led her radically to change the direction of her life, and to dedicate it to him. She wrote of this and of subsequent mystical experiences in *The Herald of Divine Love*, also known as her *Revelations*. Toward the end of her life she composed the *Exercises*, seven retreat experiences consisting of prayers, personal reflections, and instructions designed for her own as well as others' use.

Gertrude drew inspiration from the Bible and the liturgy, both of which she loved. She saw no conflict between her own prayer life and the prayer of the Church, seeing them instead as closely related and mutually enriching. Her sense of familiarity with Jesus, Mary and the saints resulted in a great liberty of spirit, and boundless confidence.

Gilbert of Hoyland

Very little in known for certain about Gilbert's life—not even the date and place of his birth, nor the year or place where he became a monk. He may have entered Clairvaux and been sent to England with the founders of Rievaulx in 1132. We do know that he was on terms of close friendship with Aelred of Rievaulx. When, in 1147, the monastic congregation of Savigny was incorporated into the Cistercian Order, Gilbert in all likelihood was sent to the savigniac house at Swineshead, Lincolnshire to aid the monks there in adopting the cistercian way of life. He remained there as abbot until his death in 1172.

It may have been Gilbert's great admiration for Bernard of Clairvaux that inspired him to continue the great abbot's commentary *On the Song of Songs*; or he may have been appointed to do so. His series of forty-seven sermons combine the practical and the mystical, and the spiritual journey is presented with grace and a flair for apt comparison.

Guerric of Igny

Born at Tournai, in modern Belgium, about 1080, Guerric was probably educated, and may have taught, at the cathedral school there. For a time he lived as a solitary in a small house near the church. Attracted by the reputation of Bernard, he went to Clairvaux, probably in 1125, and at Bernard's urging, became a monk. In 1138 he was elected second abbot of Igny, a daughter house of Clairvaux—and mother house of Signy, where William was a monk. He governed it until his death in 1157. As abbot, he preached to his community on the occasion of the principal feasts of the church year. Fifty-four of these *Liturgical Sermons* have come down to us. They present the stages of Christ's earthly life as a model for those who aspire to imitate him, as well as giving valuable advice, simple and sober, yet profound, on following the path to God.

Isaac of Stella

The details of Isaac's life are uncertain. He was born probably about 1100 in England. As a young man he went to France, where he studied philosophy and theology, perhaps at Paris or Chartres. Around 1140, he entered a cistercian monastery, probably Pontigny, south of Paris. He was made abbot of Stella, near Poitiers, in 1147. There he received the exiled archbishop of Canterbury, Thomas Becket, in January 1165. About 1167, Isaac, with a few other monks, retired to the island of Ré off the Atlantic coast, where they lived in great solitude and poverty. A number of the *Sermons on the Liturgical Year* which have come down to us seem to have been preached to his monks there. Isaac probably returned to Stella before he died, sometime after 1174.

More speculative than the other Cistercians represented in this book, the scholarly Isaac was an original and powerful thinker. Yet he combined his great interest in philosophical questions with a deep monastic spirit, and a particularly strong awareness of the unity of Christ and Christians in the Church, the mystical body of Christ.

John of Forde

John was born in the mid 1140s, probably in Devonshire, England. He entered Forde as a young man. He was prior (second in command) under Abbot Baldwin until the monks of Bindon in Dorset chose him to be their abbot. After Baldwin's death, John was elected abbot of Forde, and governed it until his death in 1214.

Despite feelings of inadequacy, John took up the commentary *On the Song of Songs* where Bernard of Clairvaux and Gilbert of Hoyland had left off. In one hundred twenty sermons marked by his ardent spirit and deep personal love for Jesus, he brought the commentary to its conclusion.

William of Saint Thierry

Born in Liège, Belgium, perhaps about 1085, William studied at the cathedral school, probably of Rheims, perhaps at Laon. He became a Benedictine monk at the abbey of Saint Nicasius at Rheims; about 1119 he was elected abbot of the nearby monastery of Saint Thierry, and became a leading figure in the renewal of benedictine monastic life. At about this time he visited Clairvaux and formed a lasting friendship with Bernard, one which deeply influenced both men. Long attracted to the cistercian way of life, William resigned his abbacy in 1135, and entered Signy, a granddaughter house of Clairvaux, where he remained as a simple monk for the rest of his life.

While at Saint Thierry William wrote his treatises *On the Nature and Dignity of Love*, *On Contemplating God* and twelve of his thirteen *Meditations*. Among the works written or completed at Signy are his *Brief Commentary on the Song of Songs*, a longer *Exposition on the Song of Songs*, and *The Mirror of Faith*. Perhaps his most important, and certainly his most wide-spread, work is the long letter to the Carthusian monks of Mont-Dieu, describing the journey to God, and known as *The Golden*

Epistle. William's spirituality has a warm, affective character but it rests on a solid and carefully articulated doctrinal basis. He has a rich teaching on the Trinity, with special emphasis on the role of the Holy Spirit.

Let your voice sound in my ears,

good Jesus,

that my heart may learn how to love you,

my mind how to love you,

the inmost being of my soul how to love you.

Aelred of Rievaulx[1]

---

1. *The Mirror of Charity* 1.1.2; CF 17:88

Bibliography ∾

All books, unless otherwise noted, are published in The Cistercian Fathers Series (CF) and The Cistercian Studies Series (CS) by Cistercian Publications, Kalamazoo MI.-Spencer, MA. When the book title is not the same as the title of the work quoted, the book title has been supplied.

Aelred of Rievaulx

Jesus at the Age of Twelve. Translated by Theodore Berkeley OCSO. CF 2. *Aelred of Rievaulx: Treatises I*. (1971).
The Mirror of Charity. Translated by Elizabeth Connor OCSO. CF 17. (1990).
Rule for a Recluse. Translated by M. Paul Macpherson OCSO. CF 2. *Aelred of Rievaulx: Treatises I* (1971).
Spiritual Friendship. Translated by M. Eugenia Laker SSND. CF 5. (1974).

Anonymous

'The Spirit and the Soul'. Translated by Erasmo Leiva and Benedicta Ward SLG, in *Three Treatises on Man*. CF 24 (1977)

Baldwin of Forde

Baldwin of Ford: Spiritual Tractates [abbreviated
    Tractate]. Translated by David N. Bell. CF 38, 41.
    (1986).

Beatrice of Nazareth

The Life of Beatrice of Nazareth. Translated by Roger De
    Ganck OCSO. CF 50. (1991).
'The Seven Modes of Loving'. Translated by Michael
    Casey OCSO, in *Tjurunga* [Australia] No. 50. Also
    translated in *The Life of Beatrice of Nazareth*, pp.
    288–331.

Bernard of Clairvaux

Sermons On the Song of Songs. Translated by Kilian
    Walsh OCSO and Irene Edmonds. CF 4, 7, 31, 40.
Bernard of Clairvaux: On the Song of Songs. 4 volumes
    (1971, 1976, 1979, 1980).
The Steps of Humility and Pride. Translated by
    M. Ambrose Conway OCSO. CF 13. (1989).
On Loving God. Translated by Robert Walton OSB. CF 13.
    (1974, 1995).
On Grace and Free Choice. Translated by Daniel
    O'Donovan OCSO. CF 19. (1988).
Sermon On Conversion. Translated by Marie-Bernard
    Saïd OSB. CF 25. *Bernard of Clairvaux: Sermons on
    Conversion* (1981).
Sermons on Psalm 90. Translated by Marie-Bernard Saïd
    OSB. CF 25 *Sermons on Conversion* (1981).
Five Books on Consideration. Translated by John D.
    Anderson and Elizabeth T. Kennan. CF 37. (1976).
*Sermons for the Christmas Season: Advent, Christmas
    and Purification.* Translated by Irene Edmonds. CF
    51. (Forthcoming).

Sermons for the Summer Season. Translated by Beverly Kienzle. CF 53. (1991).

Letters. Translated by Bruno Scott James. CF 62. (1998. Originally published in 1953).

Occasional Sermons. Translated by Conrad Greenia ocso and Hugh McCaffery ocso. CF 68. (Forthcoming).

Gertrud of Helfta

The Spiritual Exercises. Translated by Gertrud Jaron Lewis and Jack Lewis. CF 49. (1989).

Gilbert of Hoyland

Sermons on the Song of Songs. Translated by Lawrence C. Braceland sj. CF 14, 20, 26. (1978, 1979).

Guerric of Igny

Liturgical Sermons. Translated by Monks of Mount Saint Bernard Abbey. CF 8, 31. (1970, 1971).

Isaac of Stella

Sermons on the Christian Year. Translated by Hugh McCaffery ocso. CF 11, 66. (1979, forthcoming).

John of Ford[e]

Sermons on the Final Verses of the Song of Songs. Translated by Wendy Mary Beckett. CF 29, 39, 43–47. (1977–1984).

William of Saint-Thierry

On Contemplating God. Translated by Penelope
Lawson csmv. CF 3. *William of Saint Thierry: On
Contemplating God, Prayer, Meditations* (1970).
Meditations. Translated by Penelope Lawson csmv. CF 3.
Exposition on the Song of Songs. Translated by
M. Columba Hart osb. CF 6. (1970).
The Golden Epistle. Translated by Theodore Berkeley
ocso. CF 12. (1971).
The Mirror of Faith. Translated by Thomas X. Davis
ocso. CF 15 (1979).
The Nature and Dignity of Love. Translated by Thomas X.
Davis ocso. CF 30. (1981).
A Brief Commentary on the Song of Songs. Translated by
Denys Turner in *Eros and Allegory.* CS 156. (1995).

CISTERCIAN TEXTS

Bernard of Clairvaux

- Apologia to Abbot William
- Five Books on Consideration: Advice to a Pope
- Homilies in Praise of the Blessed Virgin Mary
- Letters of Bernard of Clairvaux / by B.S. James
- Life and Death of Saint Malachy the Irishman
- Love without Measure: Extracts from the Writings of St Bernard / by Paul Dimier
- On Grace and Free Choice
- On Loving God / Analysis by Emero Stiegman
- Parables and Sentences
- Sermons for the Summer Season
- Sermons on Conversion
- Sermons on the Song of Songs I–IV
- The Steps of Humility and Pride

William of Saint Thierry

- The Enigma of Faith
- Exposition on the Epistle to the Romans
- Exposition on the Song of Songs
- The Golden Epistle
- The Mirror of Faith
- The Nature and Dignity of Love
- On Contemplating God: Prayer & Meditations

Aelred of Rievaulx

- Dialogue on the Soul
- Liturgical Sermons, I
- The Mirror of Charity
- Spiritual Friendship
- Treatises I: On Jesus at the Age of Twelve, Rule for a Recluse, The Pastoral Prayer
- Walter Daniel: The Life of Aelred of Rievaulx

John of Ford

- Sermons on the Final Verses of the Songs of Songs I–VII

Gilbert of Hoyland

- Sermons on the Songs of Songs I–III
- Treatises, Sermons and Epistles

Other Early Cistercian Writers

- Adam of Perseigne, Letters of
- Alan of Lille: The Art of Preaching
- Amadeus of Lausanne: Homilies in Praise of Blessed Mary
- Baldwin of Ford: Spiritual Tractates I–II
- Geoffrey of Auxerre: On the Apocalypse
- Gertrud the Great: Spiritual Exercises
- Gertrud the Great: The Herald of God's Loving-Kindness (Books 1, 2)

- Gertrud the Great: The Herald of God's Loving-Kindness (Book 3)
- Guerric of Igny: Liturgical Sermons Vol. 1 & 2
- Helinand of Froidmont: Verses on Death
- Idung of Prüfening: Cistercians and Cluniacs: The Case for Cîteaux
- Isaac of Stella: Sermons on the Christian Year, I–[II]
- The Life of Beatrice of Nazareth
- The School of Love. An Anthology of Early Cistercian Texts
- Serlo of Wilton & Serlo of Savigny: Seven Unpublished Works
- Stephen of Lexington: Letters from Ireland
- Stephen of Sawley: Treatises

MONASTIC TEXTS

Eastern Monastic Tradition

- Besa: The Life of Shenoute
- Cyril of Scythopolis: Lives of the Monks of Palestine
- Dorotheos of Gaza: Discourses and Sayings
- Evagrius Ponticus: Praktikos and Chapters on Prayer
- Handmaids of the Lord: Lives of Holy Women in Late Antiquity & the Early Middle Ages / by Joan Petersen
- Harlots of the Desert / by Benedicta Ward
- John Moschos: The Spiritual Meadow
- Lives of the Desert Fathers
- Lives of Simeon Stylites / by Robert Doran
- Mena of Nikiou: Isaac of Alexandra & St Macrobius
- The Monastic Rule of Iosif Volotsky (Revised Edition) / by David Goldfrank
- Pachomian Koinonia I–III (Armand Veilleux)
- Paphnutius: Histories/Monks of Upper Egypt
- The Sayings of the Desert Fathers / by Benedicta Ward
- The Spiritually Beneficial Tales of Paul, Bishop of Monembasia / by John Wortley
- Symeon the New Theologian: TheTheological and Practical Treatises & The Three Theological Discourses / by Paul McGuckin
- Theodoret of Cyrrhus: A History of the Monks of Syria
- The Syriac Fathers on Prayer and the Spiritual Life / by Sebastian Brock

Western Monastic Tradition

- Anselm of Canterbury: Letters I–III / by Walter Fröhlich
- Bede: Commentary…Acts of the Apostles
- Bede: Commentary…Seven Catholic Epistles

CISTERCIAN PUBLICATIONS

TITLES LISTING

- Bede: Homilies on the Gospels I–II
- Bede: Excerpts from the Works of St Augustine on the Letters of the Blessed Apostle Paul
- The Celtic Monk / by U. Ó Maidín
- Life of the Jura Fathers
- Peter of Celle: Selected Works
- Letters of Rancé I–II
- Rule of the Master
- Rule of Saint Augustine

Christian Spirituality

- The Cloud of Witnesses: The Development of Christian Doctrine / by David N. Bell
- The Call of Wild Geese / by Matthew Kelty
- The Cistercian Way / by André Louf
- The Contemplative Path
- Drinking From the Hidden Fountain / by Thomas Spidlík
- Eros and Allegory: Medieval Exegesis of the Song of Songs / by Denys Turner
- Fathers Talking / by Aelred Squire
- Friendship and Community / by Brian McGuire
- Gregory the Great: Forty Gospel Homilies
- High King of Heaven / by Benedicta Word
- The Hermitage Within / by a Monk
- Life of St Mary Magdalene and of Her Sister St Martha / by David Mycoff
- A Life Pleasing to God / by Augustine Holmes
- The Luminous Eye / by Sebastian Brock
- Many Mansions / by David N. Bell
- Mercy in Weakness / by André Louf
- The Name of Jesus / by Irénée Hausherr
- No Moment Too Small / by Norvene Vest
- Penthos: The Doctrine of Compunction in the Christian East / by Irénée Hausherr
- Praying the Word / by Enzo Bianchi
- Rancé and the Trappist Legacy / by A. J. Krailsheimer
- Russian Mystics / by Sergius Bolshakoff
- Sermons in a Monastery / by Matthew Kelty
- Silent Herald of Unity: The Life of Maria Gabrielle Sagheddu / by Martha Driscoll
- Spiritual Direction in the Early Christian East / by Irénée Hausherr
- The Spirituality of the Christian East / by Thomas Spidlík
- The Spirituality of the Medieval West / by André Vauchez
- The Spiritual World of Isaac the Syrian / by Hilarion Alfeyev
- Tuning In To Grace / by André Louf
- Wholly Animals: A Book of Beastly Tales / by David N. Bell

MONASTIC STUDIES

- Community and Abbot in the Rule of St Benedict I–II / by Adalbert de Vogüé
- The Finances of the Cistercian Order in the Fourteenth Century / by Peter King
- Fountains Abbey and Its Benefactors / by Joan Wardrop
- The Hermit Monks of Grandmont / by Carole A. Hutchison
- In the Unity of the Holy Spirit / by Sighard Kleiner
- A Life Pleasing to God: Saint Basil's Monastic Rules / By Augustine Holmes
- The Joy of Learning & the Love of God: Essays in Honor of Jean Leclercq
- Monastic Odyssey / by Marie Kervingant
- Monastic Practices / by Charles Cummings
- The Occupation of Celtic Sites in Ireland / by Geraldine Carville
- Reading St Benedict / by Adalbert de Vogüé
- Rule of St Benedict: A Doctrinal and Spiritual Commentary / by Adalbert de Vogüé
- The Rule of St Benedict / by Br. Pinocchio
- The Spiritual World of Isaac the Syrian / by Hilarion Alfeyev
- St Hugh of Lincoln / by David H. Farmer
- The Venerable Bede / by Benedicta Ward
- Western Monasticism / by Peter King
- What Nuns Read / by David N. Bell
- With Greater Liberty: A Short History of Christian Monasticism & Religious Orders / by Karl Frank

Cistercian Studies

- Aelred of Rievaulx: A Study / by Aelred Squire
- Athirst for God: Spiritual Desire in Bernard of Clairvaux's Sermons on the Song of Songs / by Michael Casey
- Beatrice of Nazareth in Her Context / by Roger De Ganck
- Bernard of Clairvaux: Man, Monk, Mystic / by Michael Casey [tapes and readings]
- Bernardus Magister...Nonacentenary
- Catalogue of Manuscripts in the Obrecht Collection of the Institute of Cistercian Studies / by Anna Kirkwood
- Christ the Way: The Christology of Guerric of Igny / by John Morson
- The Cistercians in Denmark / by Brian McGuire
- The Cistercians in Scandinavia / by James France
- A Difficult Saint / by Brian McGuire

- A Gathering of Friends: Learning & Spirituality in John of Ford / by Costello and Holdsworth
- Image and Likeness: Augustinian Spirituality of William of St Thierry / by David Bell
- Index of Authors & Works in Cistercian Libraries in Great Britain I / by David Bell
- Index of Cistercian Authors and Works in Medieval Library Catalogues in Great Britian / by David Bell
- The Mystical Theology of St Bernard / by Étienne Gilson
- The New Monastery: Texts & Studies on the Earliest Cistercians
- Nicolas Cotheret's Annals of Cîteaux / by Louis J. Lekai
- Pater Bernhardus: Martin Luther and Saint Bernard / by Franz Posset
- Pathway of Peace / by Charles Dumont
- A Second Look at Saint Bernard / by Jean Leclercq
- The Spiritual Teachings of St Bernard of Clairvaux / by John R. Sommerfeldt
- Studies in Medieval Cistercian History
- Studiosorum Speculum / by Louis J. Lekai
- Three Founders of Cîteaux / by Jean-Baptiste Van Damme
- Towards Unification with God (Beatrice of Nazareth in Her Context, 2)
- William, Abbot of St Thierry
- Women and St Bernard of Clairvaux / by Jean Leclercq

MEDIEVAL RELIGIOUS WOMEN

edited by Lillian Thomas Shank and John A. Nichols:
- Distant Echoes
- Hidden Springs: Cistercian Monastic Women (2 volumes)
- Peace Weavers

CARTHUSIAN TRADITION

- The Call of Silent Love / by A Carthusian
- The Freedom of Obedience / by A Carthusian
- From Advent to Pentecost / by A Carthusian
- Guigo II: The Ladder of Monks & Twelve Meditations / by E. Colledge & J. Walsh
- Halfway to Heaven / by R.B. Lockhart
- Interior Prayer / by A Carthusian
- Meditations of Guigo II / by A. Gordon Mursall
- The Prayer of Love and Silence / by A Carthusian
- Poor, Therefore Rich / by A Carthusian
- They Speak by Silences / by A Carthusian
- The Way of Silent Love (A Carthusian Miscellany)

- Where Silence is Praise / by A Carthusian
- The Wound of Love (A Carthusian Miscellany)

CISTERCIAN ART, ARCHITECTURE & MUSIC

- Cistercian Abbeys of Britain
- Cistercians in Medieval Art / by James France
- Studies in Medieval Art and Architecture / edited by Meredith Parsons Lillich (Volumes II–V are now available)
- Stones Laid Before the Lord / by Anselme Dimier
- Treasures Old and New: Nine Centuries of Cistercian Music (compact disc and cassette)

THOMAS MERTON

- The Climate of Monastic Prayer / by T. Merton
- Legacy of Thomas Merton / by P. Hart
- Message of Thomas Merton / by P. Hart
- Monastic Journey of Thomas Merton / by P. Hart
- Thomas Merton/Monk / by P. Hart
- Thomas Merton on St Bernard
- Toward an Integrated Humanity / edited by M. Basil Pennington

CISTERCIAN LITURGICAL DOCUMENTS SERIES

- Cistercian Liturgical Documents Series / edited by Chrysogonus Waddell, ocso
- Hymn Collection of the...Paraclete
- Institutiones nostrae: The Paraclete Statutes
- Molesme Summer-Season Breviary (4 volumes)
- Old French Ordinary & Breviary of the Abbey of the Paraclete (2 volumes)
- Twelfth-century Cistercian Hymnal (2 volumes)
- The Twelfth-century Cistercian Psalter
- Two Early Cistercian Libelli Missarum

STUDIA PATRISTICA

- Studia Patristica XVIII, Volumes 1, 2 and 3

CISTERCIAN PUBLICATIONS

HOW TO CONTACT US

Editorial Offices & Customer Service

- **Cistercian Publications**
  WMU Station 1201 Oliver Street
  Kalamazoo, Michigan 49008   USA

  Telephone 616 387 8920
  Fax   616 387 8390
  e-mail   cistpub@wmich.edu

Canada

- **Novalis**
  49 Front Street East, Second Floor
  Toronto, Ontario M5E 1B3

  Telephone 1 800 204 4140
  Fax   416 363 9409

U.K.

- **Cistercian Publications UK**
  Mount Saint Bernard Abbey
  Coalville, Leicester LE67 5UL

- **UK Customer Service & Book Orders**
  Cistercian Publications
  97 Loughborough Road
  Thringstone, Coalville
  Leicester LE67 8LQ

  Telephone 01530 45 27 24
  Fax   01530 45 02 10
  e-mail   MsbcistP@aol.com

Website & Warehouse

- **www.spencerabbey.org/cistpub**

- **Book Returns (prior permission)**
  Cistercian Publications
  Saint Joseph's Abbey
  167 North Spencer Road
  Spencer MA 01562-1233   USA

  Telephone 508 885 8730
  Fax   508 885 4687
  e-mail   cistpub@spencerabbey.org

Trade Accounts & Credit Applications

- **Cistercian Publications / Accounting**
  6219 West Kistler Road
  Ludington, MI 49431   USA

  Fax   231 843 8919

Cistercian Publications is a non-profit corporation. Its publishing program is restricted to monastic texts in translation and books on the monastic tradition.

A complete catalogue of texts in translation and studies on early, medieval, and modern monasticism is available, free of charge, from any of the addresses above.